Career Alchemy

An Inside Out Approach to Joy, Success & Fulfilment Through Work

Dr Ramya Ranganathan

Verses Kindler Publication.

Website: www.verseskindlerpublication.com

———————————————————

© Copyright, 2024, Dr. Ramya Ranganathan

Career Alchemy-An Inside Out Approach to Joy, Success, and Fulfilment through Work

By: Dr. Ramya Ranganathan

ISBN: 978-93-5605-700-5

NON-FICTION STORIES 1st Edition

Price: INR 499/ $20

The opinions/ contents expressed in this book are solely of the author and do not represent the opinions/ standings/ thoughts of PUBLISHER.

Disclaimer

Career Alchemy-An Inside Out Approach to Joy, Success, and Fulfilment through Work is written by Dr. Ramya Ranganathan.

The published work is the original contents of the author and she has done her best to edit and make it error-free.

The opinions/ contents expressed in this book are solely of the author and do not represent the opinions/ standings/ thoughts of the publisher. Any resemblance of names of actual person, place or institute is purely coincidental to carry forward the story.

The write-up is the original content of the author and the author is solely responsible for it, the publisher would not be responsible for it.

To

All Divine Sources & Forces
Inside & Outside of Us

May we get freedom from
Ignorance, Brainwashing & Fear

May we leave behind patterns of
Insecurity, Helplessness & Hopelessness

And May We Embrace
Love, Light & Courage

Embodying & Becoming Channels
For
Beauty, Abundance, Joy & Harmony

In Our Work
&
In Our Lives
&
In Communion with Our Beloved Planet Earth

Contents

Introduction: From Pain to Purpose

'Work'

'Job'

'Career'

These words have become the shorthand for defining who we are in today's society. They dominate our conversations and shape our perceptions of one another. We routinely ask, out of habit or curiosity, 'Where do you work?' or 'What do you do?'

However, have we ever asked the more significant question, *"Do you find contentment or happiness in your work?"* Let's forget about others and focus within; have we ever sincerely asked this question to ourselves?

The relationship between people and their work is largely unexplored territory. And why this is so can be adeptly understood through my own experience. Having my resume graced with the crowning jewels of degrees from IIT Madras and IIM Ahmedabad, I had my fair share of highly sought-after jobs. Good money, reputed companies, and jobs worthy of my education; I thought all boxes had been checked and that I would flourish in them.

But the reality was marked by immense frustration, dissatisfaction, and a nagging doubt of not fitting in. Now, if you've been lucky enough to never be in this state, you might be thinking, *"Everyone faces some difficulties or has bad days at work. You just have to power through it."*

But what I was facing went beyond this and 'powering through' was simply not an option that I wanted to consider.

The first blow came when my work made me question my own efficiency, something I deeply value. Right from my school days, I had been very performance focussed. Every time I cracked a tough problem, it felt like I'd won a mental challenge, delivering that satisfying rush of dopamine. I approached my exams like a game that could not only challenge me intellectually, but also boost my self-esteem during my awkward teenage years, getting me the praise I desperately sought from family, teachers, and friends.

What I have realized in hindsight is that I had felt secure in subjects like Math and Physics because of the predictability that they brought to my world. My performance was totally in my control! If I asked two numbers to add up - they ALWAYS added up in the very same way. If a trolley rolled down a slope, it would ALWAYS accelerate at a pace I could calculate with a formula.

So, it was no surprise that operations management became my favorite subject during my MBA—and I entered the corporate world determined to transform it into a model of efficiency. Unfortunately though, I approached the corporate environment with a rigid engineering mindset, expecting people to function as smoothly, and transparently as machines.

Obviously, they did not and it bothered me immensely.

I became increasingly frustrated with the inefficiencies and delays caused by interpersonal friction, power plays, and complex people dynamics that occur in organizations. This external inefficiency mirrored an internal struggle, manifesting as feelings of personal ineffectiveness. My brain was no longer getting the dopamine highs that it had grown accustomed to from the 'predictable wins' of exams. I started feeling inadequate and dissatisfied and began to see myself as a failure.

Then came the Monday morning blues, but instead of being restricted to just Monday mornings, my blues were relentless and persisted throughout the week. Waking up and going to work every day became a battle that eventually took its toll to suck the liveliness out of me and make me feel hollow. I felt like a zombie drifting through my own life.

I tried changing jobs, tried changing cities, but no matter what, my inner experience of work stayed the same. My list of complaints and frustrations only grew longer. I found myself grappling with questions I had never asked before:

"Why did I need to work, was it only for the money?"

"Why did I feel so disconnected from my job?"

"Would I ever find joy and fulfilment in my career?"

I tried discussing these things with the people around me. I was fortunate that many were willing to listen, but unfortunate that none of their advice offered a way out. Some simply couldn't understand why I was unhappy with such a high-paying job. Others made me feel guilty, accusing me of not trying hard enough. And still, others urged me to wait it out, assuring me that I'd eventually 'settle' or 'adjust,' just as they had.

Then one day, a conversation with a teacher changed everything. She listened patiently as I vented, letting me run through my long list of complaints. When I finally finished, she looked at me and said, *"Ramya, the real questions in your head are about the relationship between humans and work. You should study that."*

Her words stopped me in my tracks. Something about her suggestion felt light and expansive, cutting through the fog of my mental chatter. She had taken all my chaotic complaints, identified the patterns, and distilled the essence of my frustration into a question. And she was spot on.

My constant discontent wasn't just about my personal blues; it was a deeper inquiry into why I felt so disconnected from my work. My frustrations with the irrational, seemingly unfair, and politically charged behavior I saw in the workplace were really questions about human behavior—about people dynamics at work.

I took up the challenge, little knowing that this very quest would actually grow into my life's work. I explored these topics as a scientist (getting a PhD in Organizational Behaviour from London Business School en route), as a philosopher (immersing myself in the study and understanding of the Bhagavad Gita and Buddhist Philosophy), and as an artist (painting and sculpting on the canvas of my life itself).

What I discovered through my research, studies, and experimentations was something that would transform not just my own work life but the work life of thousands in the coming years. I realized that work as an activity contains within it elements that can make it either our greatest problem or our greatest blessing.

You can observe the evidence of this for yourself – just look around at the people in your life. For some, work is a source of immense stress—something they endure to make money and then use to get through life. For others (albeit a select few), work is a joyful and meaningful part of their existence, naturally aligning with who they are and how they want to live.

I continued to study and research on what creates this huge variance in how people experience their work. I began to explore whether we could consciously shape our career experiences rather than leave them to chance. Could we develop a structured approach to make work more fulfilling and enjoyable? Imagine the excitement you feel when you put on your sports gear and get ready to play. I was curious to uncover what could make us feel that way when we set out to work on a Monday morning.

My formal studies in psychology opened me up to the role that our internal narratives can play in our happiness and motivation, but it wasn't until I started meditating that I became acutely aware of just how influential the mental chatter in our minds can be. My wake-up call came during a Vipassana retreat in Herefordshire. For ten days, we maintained complete silence—not a word spoken, no eye contact with other participants, no phones, no distractions, not even a pen or paper to jot down a thought.

It was just me and my mind, and that's when I discovered the rich, tangled world of my thoughts. I was stunned by how much of it was sheer junk—repetitive, outdated, petty thoughts marching in uninvited, masquerading as meaningful. I found myself irritated, even amused, but mostly I felt a surge of determination. I realized it was time to stop letting my mind blindly run the show and start taking back control.

The more I researched, the more I realized that to truly transform our external work experience, we first need to do some serious internal work on our own brains. We have to start reprogramming and reshaping the mental models we've been conditioned with—about success, failure, work, leisure, money, freedom, choice, happiness, strengths, weaknesses, and a few other things. This inner reprogramming is just as crucial (if not more so) than the external aspects of career selection and fit.

I began to see that most career coaching programs out there focus almost exclusively on the outer activity—choosing work that aligns with our strengths and interests. Some even help us find alignment with our core values and purpose. While these are undoubtedly important components of career crafting (and ones I include in my coaching as well), they're incomplete without doing the inner work of reprogramming our brains' limiting mental models and beliefs.

In fact, when you combine outer work with inner work, each enhances the other's effectiveness in ways that can seem almost magical and transformational. That's what inspired me to create a unique career crafting process that integrates both inner work and outer work.

My first program in this space was a course called 'Personal Values, Goals, and Career Options' at IIM Bangalore. Building on that, I developed another program for working executives called 'Leading with Joy,' as well as an online course titled 'Crafting Realities – Work, Happiness, and Meaning,' which was offered to a global audience across 16 countries on EdX. I then started conducting corporate workshops (tailoring content to meet specific client needs), eventually training over 50,000 people over the course of 15 years.

I also began one-on-one coaching, which gave me the privilege of diving deep into the inner worlds of my clients. Learning from their journeys, along with insights from my research and workshops, I started curating online cohort-based programs to help people redesign their careers. The most updated version of this work is now what I call 'Career Alchemy.'

Based on my experience with all my past participants and clients, I can confidently say this: No matter who you are, and no matter what your current 'job' or 'work' or 'life situation' is, it's never too late to recraft and alchemize your career. In fact, the older you are and the richer your portfolio of experiences, the more colors and shades you have to paint and sculpt your future with. I've had people over sixty in my workshops, and they've discovered completely new career possibilities by following this inside-out approach.

The journey you will embark on with this book is not about finding a 'one right career' as an answer to the problem of your life. Far from that - it will be an ongoing journey of discovery, creating, experimenting and choosing. You will be more of a sculptor, and less of a seeker in this process.

Let me take you on a little tour of what's inside this book. In Chapter 1, we start by building a strong foundation of inner sovereignty. Why do we begin here? Because I want you to experience true transformation, not just tiny steps forward. And the magic lies in the inner work—mastering your thoughts, emotions, and reshaping those mental models and beliefs that have been silently steering your life.

In Chapter 2, we'll dive into the Hero Mindset. Trust me, it's more than just a mindset; it's a way of living that brings out your inner champion! Then, in Chapters 3, 4, and 5, we'll take a good, hard look at the big trio—Success, Work, and Money. Together, we'll redefine what these mean to you so they become empowering frames to craft your career with.

Moving on to Chapter 6, we learn to manage our brains—because let's face it, stress and multitasking can really mess with our mojo! I'll show you how to get your mind clear and focused, even on the craziest days. In Chapter 7, we learn to cultivate resilience and navigate failures with grace, because life is full of twists and turns, and you, my friend, are stronger than you know.

Chapter 8 will help you make friends with those inner voices—the cheerleaders and the critics—so you can channel them to your advantage. Chapter 9 is about owning your unique strengths and quirks, because those are what make you, YOU! We'll dig deep to uncover your unique gifts and learn to leverage them with confidence.

Then, in Chapter 10, we'll get into the art of goal-setting—using this powerful tool to move forward without letting it become a stressor. In Chapter 11, we'll explore the possibilities of a portfolio career—perfect for those of us who can't stick to one thing because we're interested in many things!

Career crafting is not a solo game and so in chapter 12 we shall explore how we can manage interpersonal conflicts with our peers and colleagues and in chapter 13 we explore the nuances of co-creating with energy flows, both inside and outside of ourselves.

Throughout this journey, you are the star of the show. You'll be the one crafting both your inner world and your outer career path. I'm just here to hand you the right tools and guide you with exercises that help you get started. Think of me as your cheerleader and guide, nudging you to explore, experiment, and create a career that lights you up.

You can use this book in one of three ways.

Solo Journey: Read each chapter at your own pace, working through the exercises as you go.

Partner Up: Get a learning buddy or form a small Pod (a tight-knit accountability group of 2 to 4 members) and progress together. The topics and exercises in this book are designed to spark deep, meaningful conversations. Throughout the book, you'll find highlighted questions and action points perfect for your Pod meetings.

Get a Coach: This book is crafted to raise your awareness about all aspects of inner work that impact your relationship with work and career. Working with a coach can provide that extra layer of support, helping you go deeper, should you want to.

No matter how you decide to use this book, my deepest intention is to ignite a transformation in the way you approach your work and career. I want to help you break free from limiting, frustrating, or stressful patterns of the past and empower you to craft a future brimming with possibility and purpose. Remember, this journey isn't just about finding a better job—it's about crafting a joyful life and career that truly supports you to express your inner potential and create the impact that you want to in this world.

- Dr. Ramya Ranganathan
Poet | Professor | Parent | Philosopher

1

Getting Started with Inner Sovereignty

"Until you make the unconscious conscious, it will direct your life and
you will call it fate."

Carl Jung

There are innumerable experiences and occurrences that characterize and comprise the journey that we call life. As we make our way ahead, we see different sights, hear and speak about varied topics, feel a range of sensations, and interact with diverse people. We often think of these as being limited to that moment and that particular incident.

What we fail to take into account, however, is that each of these external experiences permeates to the inside too, and becomes a part of us in some way.

Every activity, interaction, or sensation (be it visual, auditory, or sensory) transforms into a compact but comprehensive database for our mind from which the mind then continues to draw and utilize information as and when relevant. Moment by moment our mind combines information from this internal database with the new information relevant to each situation, and then begins making sense of this new information.

As a simple example, when you have an 'external experience' of seeing something interesting on the road and walking toward it for a closer look, it is actually your mind rapidly processing the data given to it and making meaning out of it in real time and directing your body to walk closer. Everything that we experience on the outside can be understood and acted upon by us only after our mind deciphers and makes sense of it.

And how does our mind do so?

It leverages the art of storytelling and crafts an internal narrative to piece together the various bits of data that it gathers.

Let us take an example here. Picture yourself walking through a market, and suddenly, you're caught in a spell of rain. In terms of physical occurrences or sensations, what is happening is that water is falling from the skies and making your skin and hair wet. In terms of internal thoughts, however, a lot more is going on. Your mind can go in any one of several different directions.

You may take the course of wondering about the weather and start thinking, *"This was unexpected! Why did monsoon come so early?"* Or, you may embrace the magic of monsoon and flood yourself with happy thoughts like, *"This is so enjoyable! I love the fresh air and lush green colors that follow the rain."* Perhaps, you will regret the unexpected shower and reprimand yourself for not carrying an umbrella, or spring into action mode and profusely start thinking about how to shield yourself from the rain.

There is a single objective reality, but multiple inner dialogues and interpretations that can stem from it. We thus go through life with a constant internal chatter that narrates and tells stories of everything we perceive and experience externally. And the shocking part is how unaware we mostly are, and how blissfully ignorant we remain of these ongoings in our mind. We never stop to really think about it, or try to harness it for our own good.

My aim, however, is to navigate you towards paying a greater amount of attention to what's going on inside— how your mind is learning and making sense of things, the kind of stories it churns out, and the narratives it weaves. And once you master this, you will be able to understand your own perceptions much more comprehensively and exert greater control over your thoughts and feelings, and eventually your actions.

Not just that, once you take greater ownership of your thoughts and feelings, you can begin to actively choose and nurture what goes on inside your minds, and through that, craft and manifest the external experiences that are more in line with what you would like to experience. This is the power of inner sovereignty.

We will explore this more deeply when we discuss the self-fulfilling prophecy later in this chapter.

Before that however, let's do a hands-on exercise.

Exercise #1: Data Gathering

This small and seemingly simple exercise will achieve a much larger goal than you can imagine. It will enable you to spot the mental chatter and narratives that run so seamlessly on auto-pilot that we don't even realize it.

Here is what you do:

1. Set an alarm on your phone or watch to give a tiny beep after every hour.

2. Every time it sounds, do a quick check on what your thoughts were at that moment and note it down in a notebook.

Think of it as a quick and concise data entry that simply tells you the gist of what you were thinking. Continue doing this for around a week, which will give you a sizeable amount of data to work with.

The aim here is to catch your brain at unsuspecting times. This exercise is different from conventional journaling because your brain has no window of opportunity to filter its thoughts. It has no way of knowing when that beep is going to come, and hence, you're left with nothing but pure and uncensored thoughts.

And the most important bit here? Be open and non-judgmental while doing the exercise. Just tap into your inner curiosity and be genuinely inquisitive to peep and see what the churn of thoughts inside your head looks like. Doing this without any judgment, ownership, and attachment to your own thoughts is the best way to get a most honest and accurate insight into what is going on inside your head.

I recommend that you pause reading this book now and do exercise 1 for a week before proceeding further.

I have gathered my data - now what?

Now that you've gathered the data, the next step is to analyze it to uncover the habitual thought patterns your brain has developed over the years.

However, before we do that, I would like to introduce you to the theory of *sensemaking* within the human brain. Inner sovereignty is not just about being the supreme authority in our inner worlds and navigating well within it. It is also about reprogramming the parts of our mind that are working as obstacles or liabilities for us.

And in order to do this we need to understand the basics of how our inner world functions.

The Process of Sensemaking

If you see the script of a foreign language, you will be unable to draw any meaning from it. But, words of a language known to you can easily be understood. The phrase 'known to you' is the key aspect here that makes all the difference.

Our mind needs an existing model within it, on the basis of which it makes sense of the varied incoming data. And we often don't realize how dependent we are on these models.

When we see an object, and try to isolate the regions of our brain that get activated in the process, a mere 10-15% is due to the signals sent by our eyes. The remaining 85-90% is accounted for by signals coming from the memory and learning centers, i.e. things that we already know. Hence, even the simple task of identifying an object needs pre-existing knowledge of what that object looks like; ie a *mental model*. Simply put, the term mental models is used to denote the maps and frameworks and learnings we hold related to whatever we have learnt about that particular concept—be it from our experiences, interactions, or formal learning.

Sensemaking, or the process through which our brain makes sense of anything therefore relies on two parallel data sources—external information gathered by our sensory organs and internal information from our existing mental models. Our brain then combines these inputs to generate an understanding or response situation by situation.

Awareness, Perceptions, Biases & Beliefs

It is impossible for us to know all the information that is out there, or be aware of everything at all times. Take students sitting in a classroom—does their focus need to be equally divided between the lesson being taught, and peripheral items like the number of fans, desks, and light? It is clear that they need to prioritize in order to be functional and effective. This selective information that we focus on is called *bounded awareness.*

The pro? It helps channel our attention to the things that truly matter. The con? It often limits us and biases our perception of the world.

Imagine this whole process as filtering information through a sieve—it allows some things in while keeping others out. For our mind, it's like there's a lens at work—a lens of perception. This lens is shaped by our interests, beliefs, motives, agendas, and emotions. In fact, it is notorious for selectively letting in information that confirms or aligns with our beliefs, leading to what psychologists call a *confirmation bias.*

Our beliefs are way more powerful than what most people think. To give you an example, our beliefs or expectations of another person's behavior can actually influence that other person's behavior. In fact this phenomenon has been widely tested and is known as the *Pygmalion Effect.*

Our beliefs not only determine what we see and perceive, and how we unknowingly orchestrate the behaviour of others around us (through influences such as the Pygmalion Effect), but they also guide the actions we take and the choices we make. In sum total, what happens as a result is that our beliefs actually have a direct effect on how we create our lives and experience it. This leads to what is often known as the *self-fulfilling prophecy*, a phenomenon where it appears as if our beliefs are actually creating our reality.

Our Beliefs are a part of the larger system of knowledge structures in our brains, what we earlier referred to in this chapter as mental models. Knowing now that these mental models will heavily influence not only your actions and feelings but also the behavior of others, the stakes are higher than ever to thoroughly understand and upgrade your mental models—something we will be doing throughout this book!.

Managing Our Mental Models

Our brain possesses a number of mental models. But how did it acquire or form them? Were they just placed there, or is there a more elaborate system for how they came to be?

Mental models are formed through a combination of sensemaking and repetition. In fact the relationship between mental models and sensemaking is a chicken and egg story. Each creates the other.

Information from our mental models is used for sensemaking, which helps us form new inferences or beliefs, which in turn get ingrained into our mental models. It is a cyclical and ongoing process that goes back and forth.

Additionally, mental models are also reinforced through repetitions. As is a common adage in neuroscience—*neurons that fire together, wire together.* We've all experienced the potency of this method of learning right from childhood, wherein repetitions help to drill down a concept in our minds. The good news is that now this method also offers you a way to manage the strength of your beliefs and ideas.

You see, mental models, if wired in certain ways, can be limiting—trapping us in negative cycles to keep experiencing the same problems from the same problematic beliefs. However, they also have the potential to transform into pathways of growth and excellence, if moulded properly.

The power of inner work lies in the fact that we can consciously craft energizing and empowering mental models for ourselves. Mental models that will not only change the lens through which we see the world, but also help us craft internal scripts and stories that motivate us to take positive and constructive actions—which then will direct our external reality and experiences.

So, what are the best ways to create these new and helpful mental models? Affirmations, conscious repetitions, and continuous exposure to experiences that support the new beliefs that we want to imbibe.

If you would like to learn more about managing your inner worlds and working with mental models please visit https://craftingourlives.com/book-resouces/ where I have put a 14-part video course together for you. However, if you are convinced by now, on how game changing it can be to recraft your mental models, you can move on to Exercise 2.

Exercise #2: Analysis of Mental Chatter

So why, you might ask, should you conduct an analysis of the data that you collected in Exercise 1. This is because your unique data will give you insights into the 'you-specific' internal patterns of sensemaking in your own brain.

It's tough (almost impossible) to identify our mental models directly. We have to first begin to catch the patterns of sensemaking in our brains, and then through that we can decipher the underlying mental models that are driving those patterns.

The inner work that follows in the subsequent chapters will focus on recrafting several internal mental models for you. For example you will recraft mental models related to success, failure, work, money, resilience, identity, and a few others. You will also rework the way your brain connects these various concepts and makes meaning out of them. However, in order to challenge your old ways of thinking and recreate new mental models, you need to first be aware of what kinds of internal patterns are uplifting and empowering for you, and what are depleting, or disempowering.

And this awareness of being able to notice and understand the differences in patterns of mental chatter is what you will gain through doing Exercise 2 (which involves two different ways in which you will analyse your mental chatter). Please remember to be completely non-judgmental while doing these analyses. Objectively, like a researcher, sift through the data and start looking for patterns, narratives, or stories.

Analysis 1: Typically, there are 3 distinct types of dysfunctional internal stories that most of us tell ourselves. Try spotting these story outlines within the data that you gathered through exercise 1.

1. Stories of 'I'm not good enough' or variations of it that push us toward doubt and demotivation.
2. Stories of 'I should never have done that' which shackle us in chains of guilt or shame.
3. Stories of 'I'm not safe—I'm going to be harmed', that trigger our fight or flight response.

Analysis 2: Next, analyse the data of mental chatter that you gathered by using the questions below. Go back again to the raw data you collected in exercise 1 for this part of the analysis (don't re-analyse your notes from analysis 1 of looking for storylines).

- How often were your thoughts geared toward hope/joy/serenity, <u>vs</u> stress/anxiety/fear? (What was the overall ratio between these two types of thought chains?)
- How often did you mentally criticize or scold yourself? How often did you put yourself down?
- How often did you mentally criticize others or blame others for your problems?
- How often did you compare yourself with others? How did the comparison make you feel?
- How often were you in a state of gratitude or appreciation— either for yourself or for other people and situations?

<u>Exercise #3: Reflection</u>

Use the below pointers to reflect on your overall experience of doing exercises 1 and 2. You can do this through journaling, or in conversation with your Pod members if you are working through this book with others.

- What patterns could you identify in your thoughts, and how do you think these have been influencing your behavior, choices, and actions so far?
- What role do you think your internal stories play in how you experience your work and life?

Once again, as you analyse and reflect on your mental chatter notes, please remember to not judge anything you discover. Judgment will just put an end to your discovery process. Do remember that the conditioning of our brain and how it works, our default mental models, patterns, and orientations, have almost all happened without our permission. It's a combination of what we were exposed to, what we practiced or repeatedly heard in our childhood, and other circumstantial causes.

The only aim behind these exercises and the theory shared in this chapter is to put you back at the helm; to motivate you to manage your mind, to break open the prisons it creates for you and to leverage its processes so that you can begin to craft a new experience in every walk of life for yourself, including your career. This is why we call it an inner sovereignty approach, and the keys to realizing which parts of our inner worlds need resculpting, are almost always hidden in our own ongoing mental chatter. Let me give you an example.

Redefining the Mental Model of a Working Mum: When I was a little girl, my mother was a teacher, and my father had a high-pressure job at a steel plant. When I was about seven or eight, my father asked my mother to quit her job and stay home to care for us full-time. Now, my mother was already an incredible mom, even while she was working, but my sister and I were thrilled at the idea of having her all to ourselves. So, we eagerly backed my father's suggestion. Right then, at the tender age of 8, I joined the camp of 'good mothers should stay at home to look after their kids.'

My mother, ever devoted, agreed to our wishes and left her career behind. She poured all her love and attention into raising us, and in my mind, this only reinforced the idea that 'good mothers don't work outside the home'.

Fast forward 20 years, and I became a mother myself. At the time, I was two years into my PhD and had planned an eight-week maternity leave. But when my son arrived, those plans went straight out the window. My return to school kept getting pushed further and further—six months, one year, a year and a half, and then two years. A part of me desperately wanted to go back, but my mind kept coming up with excuse after excuse. My husband, parents, and in-laws were all encouraging me to resume my studies, but I was the one putting on the brakes.

Living in London then, I'd take my son out every morning and evening to local libraries, playgroups, or parks. There, I met a group of other mothers, all stay-at-home mums like me. Over time, we became friends and would gather for chats after play sessions. During these conversations we'd often be critiquing and judging working mothers, and placing ourselves on a moral high ground. One day while walking back from one of these meets, I was tracking my own mental chatter and I realized how incredibly judgmental it had become. Unbeknownst to me, I'd divided the world of women into two camps: 'them'—the working mothers, and 'us'—the stay-at-home mums.

Once this judgment surfaced in my awareness, it wasn't rocket science to figure out why I had resorted to such extreme views. First, I had carried a belief from 20 years ago that 'you can't work and be a good mother.' Additionally, because I had given up every other activity (except being a mother), I felt the need to derive all my self-esteem from motherhood. As a result, I fiercely bought into the 'working mums are bad' narrative, so I could be the 'good mum' in comparison.

That day, I realized something powerful: as long as I held onto this 'us vs. them' mindset, criticizing working mothers, I would never give myself permission to become one. And even if I did, I wouldn't be happy and fulfilled as a working mom if my brain continued to hold working mothers in a negative light. It was time to challenge my deeply held belief and recondition my mind—or resign myself to a life where I would never work outside the home[1].

Letting go of that old belief and freeing myself from those entrenched mental models wasn't easy. But fortunately, I had a deep understanding of how our brains work (as you also now do after this chapter), and I had the tools to do the inner work necessary to rewire my thinking. Once I reworked my mental models, I was liberated to take the next step towards continuing my studies and embracing my new identity as a 'caring and loving working mother'—one that continues to create joy and motivation in my life, both in my outer world, as well as my inner world.

Affirmation Traps to Avoid

Before we close this section on working with our mental models I want to highlight an important point to keep in mind. There is a common trap that people often fall into with regard to inner work on mental models and beliefs, especially when trying to use affirmations—deliberate mental repetitions of a chosen new phrase or belief. The trap is when we create an affirmation that sounds absurd or blatantly untrue to our own brain when we think of it.

It is theoretically possible to build a belief where there is no existing data or proof of the idea in your own brain. You might come across other teachers and coaches who might advocate this

---

[1] I want to clarify that I am not saying that being a stay-at-home mum is a 'lesser option' for everyone. It can be a beautiful option when it comes from a place of true choice. In my case however, a part of me really felt called to work and so I had to examine what was holding me back.

approach as well, but I do not recommend it. Why? Because even though there is a small chance of success, the risk of a backlash (in your own thoughts) is higher and you might spend a lot of time and effort doing affirmations and either see no results or experience a negative result (because of the backlash of doubting thoughts that get triggered every time you repeat your new affirmation).

This is why in my workshops when I get people to redefine concepts like success, failure, work and money, I don't present them with pre-defined empowering definitions. I first take them (and their brain) through exercises where their own brain will actually be able to see new possibilities around these topics. Then after that, they are guided to craft their new definitions from the place of possibilities that has uniquely opened up in their own brains at that time as a result of the exercises. I further invite them to craft their new definitions in a way that is also aligned with their own values and goals. And this is the approach we follow throughout this book as well—we will first do exercises that will open your brain to possibilities and then we will leverage the power of affirmations and repetition of the newly created mental models.

Know that this process is not a one-time exercise. You can come back again a year later, and do the inner world redefinition processes again, and at that time you will open yourself up to even more possibilities than your brain allowed the previous time.

The journey of expanding the possibilities that we can experience in our lives and in our careers literally becomes an ongoing adventure. Remember though that when we use affirmations to build new mental models, we have to do the hard work of repeating them ourselves. It won't happen by itself and it cannot be outsourced or delegated. You see we are both the architect and the construction worker of our inner world project.

2

Your Career as a Hero's Journey

"This is the true joy in life, being used for a purpose recognized by yourself as a mighty one. Being a force of nature instead of a feverish, selfish little clod of ailments and grievances, complaining that the world will not devote itself to making you happy"

George Bernard Shaw

*H*ero...on hearing this term, most of us begin picturing grand entries, bulging muscles, and paparazzi. At the end of this chapter I'm hoping that instead of this, you will walk up to a mirror, look your reflection in the eye, and think, *"That's a hero!"*

Let's start with an activity here. On a piece of paper, pen down the names of two or three people that you consider heroes (think of the term 'hero' in a gender-neutral way). Don't be tempted to only think of celebrities; while they can make it to your list, try to also go deeper, even into the scope of fictional characters or people you know & interact with to bring forth the names that align with your idea of a hero.

So what is your idea of a hero? What made you choose those particular names?

The answer to these questions can uncover a very significant learning lesson. And to find them, all you need to do is reflect on the reasons or qualities that your chosen people possess, and which makes you categorize them as heroes. It is essential for you to undertake this activity by yourself, without relying on the opinions and inputs of others. Because, only then will you come face to face with the vision of a hero that feels truly heroic to you. What seems heroic to others may not be the same for you, and it is these differences that make each of us unique.

I want to invite you to own and embrace this uniqueness, and try to align your focus to the actions, behaviors, or traits that you have personally associated with the term 'hero'.

The eventual goal is to make you see yourself as the hero of your career as you craft it. And the starting point for this is identifying what comprises a hero for you. It is essential for your actions, as you alchemize and develop your career, to seem heroic to you. Because only then will your mind categorize you in the way you deserve to be seen (a hero in your own eyes).

The Hero's Journey

In the 1940s, Joseph Campbell, a scholar and mythologist, embarked on an ambitious project: to study the hero figures in mythological stories from cultures across the globe. What he uncovered was a remarkable commonality—a shared sequence of events that defined each hero's journey. Campbell identified a series of stages, or rites of passage, that nearly every protagonist experienced. He brought these patterns together into what he called the Hero's Journey.

THE HERO'S JOURNEY

But this framework is much more than just a tool for understanding ancient myths; it offers profound insights into the human experience itself. At some point in your life, you too have likely set out on a hero's journey, perhaps even more than once, without recognizing it as such. As we discussed in the previous chapter, our perceptions are shaped by the lenses through which we view the world. The Hero's Journey is one such lens—a frame that, when adopted, allows us to see the stages of our own lives with new clarity.

By looking at your life through this framework, you'll start to see familiar patterns emerging. The trials, transformations, and returns that Campbell describes are not confined to the pages of myth; they are lived experiences. In recognizing these parallels, you may find a new way to understand your personal journey—seeing yourself, perhaps for the first time, as the hero of your own life story.

Decoding the Hero Archetype

The list of qualities that you penned down in the earlier activity doubles up as a customized hero archetype, based on your own ideals, opinions, and preferences. And while I would like you to keep that unique definition of a hero in mind, I would also like to point out some common associations with the word 'hero' that are not empowering to have. If you noticed any of these associations that you have in your personal definition of a hero, you might want to drop them at this stage.

First, a hero is not someone who has to win all the time. Second, a hero is not someone who always gets grandeur and attention- a red carpet, hoards of cameras, scores of admirers, etc.

A hero is someone who goes out and takes action even when circumstances are rough, tough, or challenging. For heroes, it doesn't matter whether there are people to support or cheer them; they simply focus on the task at hand and what they must do to fulfill it. They are not people who hold unrealistic desires of having everything handled for them, or having others pander to their every request. They are not naive in believing that just because they are on a heroic mission, others will never be unkind or mean to them.

In short, a hero is an adventurer setting out on a journey full of ups and downs, successes and failures, and coming across both friends and enemies along the way.

As we take a closer look at the various stages that Joseph Campbell identified as part of the Hero's Journey, I'm going to invite you to reflect on how these stages have shown up (and will continue to appear) in your own life. I'm also going to challenge you in some places on how you might respond to these different stages.

Stages in the Hero's Journey

1. Ordinary World

The hero's journey is a cyclical one, meaning that it starts and ends at this same threshold- the ordinary world. It is simply a representation of our everyday life; our routines, our habits, our daily tasks.

There is contentment in the ordinary world and yet, we can often slip into the comfort offered by everyday familiarity, and not question the status quo.

2. Call to Adventure

Then suddenly, a jolt might come. It can be through internal or external factors. It could be triggered by the end of a relationship, getting fired from a job, or any other crisis. Alternatively, it could be the result of an epiphany or awakening that you're meant to do bigger or better things in life. This is a call to adventure.

Our minds are conditioned to favoring the 'status quo' and anything that shakes it is automatically regarded as a bad or scary thing, or a disruption. Instead, the hero's journey frame of perception allows us to 'see' jolts as an opportunity, as an invitation to embark on an adventure. And this change in viewpoint can make all the difference in how you approach the situation.

3. Refusal of the Call

"I don't want to change what I'm doing…" "I don't want to try something new…" "I'm safe where I am and I'm staying back!"

Our most natural tendency is wanting to remain in that familiarity that we're comfortable with. We want to refuse the call to adventure, and turn down the opportunity for personal growth that it offers. But sometimes, the jolt is so powerful that you're thrown from that complacent place and there's no going back. And as harsh as this sounds, it is actually life doing us a favor.

If however, you manage to say a firm *"NO!"* that refusal is going to be temporary. Life, being relentless, will eventually come knocking at your door again, the call will keep persisting till you answer. I had heard of this from my teachers and in philosophical texts, but I also learnt it the hard way in my own life—not just once but time and time again.

And hence, I'll leave you with a thought: If you must eventually answer the call (and life will ensure that you do) why try to run away from it in the first place?

4. Meeting the Mentor

The mentors you meet, the ones who inspire you to take that next bold step on your journey, can undoubtedly be an actual teacher, guru, or coach.

However, they can also be books or speeches that stir you. They can be unlikely and informal mentors like a neighbor or a boss. Even a fictional character, or a divine deity or angel can turn out playing the role of a mentor in your life—as has happened often with me.

In essence, a mentor is anyone or anything that ignites the spark of motivation in you, imparts any kind of wisdom, or guides you in the right direction.

5.   Crossing the Threshold

Think of this threshold as a boundary that separates the known from the unknown, the old from the new, and the comfortable from the uncomfortable.

It is an exciting move. However, the very wiring of our human brains means you will feel fear, anxiety, and self-doubt when stepping into the vastness of uncertainty. When this happens, just remember that it's not just you who feels this fear of the unknown and the unpredictable.

Every mythological or historical hero too has had to tackle these feelings, and summon up extraordinary amounts of courage, determination, and focus during this phase. You are in good company. And here too your mentor, whoever or whatever it may be, can help you in taking that courageous leap.

6.   Tests, Allies, Enemies

Life, much like a school or college, has a consistent set of tests laid out for you. There are unit tests, mid-term and end-term exams that we all must pass. And during these evaluations, we're surrounded by friends and enemies alike.

In the past, whenever I came across such a test or obstacle, or a person who I pictured as an enemy, I did not have the knowledge of the hero's journey to help me cope with them healthily. I would fall into a deep spiral of self-judgment and start concocting theories that either I was doing something wrong, or the universe itself was against what I had set out to do.

Now, however, I see them as facilitators. When a test or an enemy comes my way, my first thought is, *"Welcome..",* given I now understand that there isn't any hero who has not tackled these elements. I also realize that every enemy who comes my way is actually coming bearing gifts; making me stronger, cleverer, and more resilient.

The more I am understanding this phase on a deeper level, I am also realizing that not everything has to be done solo. As heroes, we can also have friends and allies who we rely upon, and trust enough to hold our hand while we're navigating challenges.

7.   Approach the Innermost Cave

The 'cave' referred to here is our inner psyche. This stage is a metaphor for revisiting and introspecting within ourselves, exploring the doubts and fears buried beneath, and allowing our limiting mental models and dysfunctional beliefs to surface into our awareness.

The innermost cave is a place we often avoid because it reveals our fears, negative emotions, and other feelings we don't like to confront. Instead, we prefer to deny their existence. But only by seeing and acknowledging them can we get closer to our inner sovereignty.

8.   The Ordeal (Death & Rebirth)

After entering the innermost cave, we become aware of the undesirable beliefs and perceptions we hold. Next, a death must occur—the death of our old self that harbored those beliefs. From here, we are reborn into a newer, more aware version of ourselves.

Like a phoenix, we rise from the ashes of our past selves and transform into a more potent and evolved version—with a new identity, upgraded mental models, an empowering mindset, and supportive belief systems.

9.   The Reward (Seizing the Force)

Along your journey, you may find external rewards - and that's wonderful. However, in my opinion, the real reward is seizing and unleashing the immense and infinite inner power that you yourself hold; the magic and force that you wield.

This phase is primarily about owning and acknowledging your inner potency and using it to achieve great things. And it is possible only because the limiting beliefs that were blocking the path of your life force have been done away with. And with its path cleared, this force will come surging ahead and empower you in ways you could have never imagined.

Your reward may also take other different forms like clarity, wisdom, fresh perspectives, new connections etc. Whatever your rewards, as a hero you will now be able to put those gifts to good use.

10. The Road Back (to the Ordinary World)

Bearing all these rewards, you begin the journey back to the ordinary world.

As the adventure draws to a close, you find yourself returning to the routine and tasks that once made up your typical day.

11. The Resurrection

Being a new person in your old settings can be confusing for you and everyone around you. Therefore, you need to integrate the two and find a way to seamlessly make them work together.

A common obstacle that arises in this phase is the mentality of the people who knew, loved, or identified with the previous version of you. They might find it difficult to reconcile the person that they knew you to be, with the person you have now become after your inner work.

It is up to you to help your loved one's get to know the 'new you' and teach them to partner with you in your empowered and upgraded version. It can be a learning journey for them as much as for you and with patient baby steps you can usually make it work.

However, occasionally you might find that someone in your life is just unwilling to accept this more powerful version of you. In such cases, you have two options in front of you. Either keep hoping and waiting for them to upgrade themselves and their models, or as painful as it may seem, you can consider letting go of such people.

12. The Return with the Elixir

Through this entire exciting journey, we learn, grow, and eventually gain wisdom and knowledge. This wisdom or knowledge can be likened to a nectar or elixir that we bring back and share with everyone.

The teachers and mentors that you might have relied upon have also shared their elixir of knowledge with you. From their mistakes, we can prevent ours. And from their experiences, we grow. Such is the power of the elixir that keeps flowing endlessly, spreading wisdom wherever it goes.

You, like most other heroes, are working toward a greater good. As you end your adventure and return with your elixir, it is going to benefit countless others. You don't need to set up a charity or foundation to help others. You could choose to do that of course, but I want you to know that just by journeying through your own challenges and emerging stronger and wiser, you have now become a presence of hope, inspiration and strength to others.

The hero's journey is a cycle, once you reintegrate back into the ordinary world .....you remain there, content, till another jolt comes to shake you into action…

Not every hero will go through each of these stages. And they might not always follow the same sequence as elaborated above. But the essence remains intact. Though every journey might take on a different form, and different sequences of stages, the overall spirit of experiencing jolts, facing challenges, learning, growing, and emerging stronger remains the same.

Exercise #1: Self Reflection

By now, you know that every hero has a journey. And if you're aiming to see yourself as the hero of your own story, it's time to recognize that you've already been on several of these journeys.

Think about your career so far: where you began, where you stand today, and where you'd like to go. That's the bigger picture, the overarching journey. Now, zoom in on a few key moments—those pivotal challenges or turning points that gave your story a new direction. These are the starting points for the smaller, meaningful journeys within your broader career path.

Pick 3 to 5 of these defining moments, and try viewing them through the lens of the hero's journey. Take some time to journal about it. Relive those events, and map them to the different stages of the hero's framework. Don't be too quick to dismiss any stage; pause, reflect, and you might find that your calls to adventure, mentors, challenges, and rewards were right there all along, just waiting to be acknowledged.

Give this exercise the time and attention it deserves. It is important to identify and acknowledge as many of the elements as you can in your past journeys, because that will give you the confidence to be open to have all these elements come into your life once again as you craft your future journey. *Just as a Hero would!*

Exercise #2: Pod Discussions

Share one or two of the sub-journeys that you have journaled about with your Pod. While doing so, ensure that you maintain the frame of a hero's journey while revisiting and narrating your own stories as well as while listening to others narrate theirs. This is important because the same incident can be viewed from different frames and that can radically alter your perception and feelings about it.

Additionally, also analyze and share the stage at which you think you are presently in your overall hero's journey of your career.

If you are not working through this book in a Pod, you can just pick one or two sub-journeys from your journaling and narrate it to a friend through a hero's journey framework.

A Hero Mindset

Having revisited your past through the Hero's Journey Framework, it's time now to turn our focus forward. So what is a magic potion that can really fuel you in your future quests as a Hero? Quite simply, it is a *Hero mindset*. The mindset that allows you to take on challenges, grow through adversity, and ultimately transform not just your career but your entire life.

The Pod is about embracing the unknown with courage, knowing that every challenge is an opportunity for growth. It's about resilience—pushing through setbacks and understanding that failure is a stepping stone, not a dead end. It's about vision— keeping your eyes on the bigger picture, the purpose that fuels your journey, even when the path is unclear. And above all, it's about self-belief—trusting in your ability to navigate your own unique journey, no matter how daunting the road ahead may seem. This mindset is already present in all of us to some extent, but it doesn't always occupy the driving seat of our mind.

Each of the following chapters in this book will help you with inner work to cultivate and nurture your Hero Mindset further, and begin to start making it a powerful default in your inner world.

However, before we embark on that, I want to introduce one additional mindset (a growth mindset) that will be a great addition to your heroes mindset. I also want to contrast a Hero Mindset with four other common mindsets that we will need to look out for along the way.

Growth Mindset

While a growth mindset can integrate extremely well with a Hero Mindset, not all the heroes we see in stories and mythology have reflected this integration. This is why I want to separately explain this mindset to you. The best way however to understand a growth mindset is to look at its opposite—a fixed mindset.

Picture a fixed mindset as wearing blinders that limit your view of what you can achieve. When you have a fixed mindset, you believe your abilities and intelligence are set in stone. You're either good at something or you're not—there's no room for improvement. This mindset can be particularly limiting in your career crafting journey. It makes you resistant to change and defensive when faced with feedback. Instead of seeing opportunities to grow, you might find yourself stuck, constantly blaming external factors for your challenges rather than looking inward.

On the other hand, a growth mindset is all about believing that you can develop your abilities through effort, learning, and persistence. With this mindset, you see challenges as opportunities, not threats. Feedback becomes a tool for growth rather than something to fear. You're more open to trying new things, learning from mistakes, and continuously improving.

This shift in perspective makes you adaptable and resilient. Instead of being stuck in a loop of blaming external factors, you start to see how you can change from the inside. You become curious about what you can learn and how you can grow. This mindset is incredibly empowering because it puts you in control of your own development, and this is also the mindset that lends itself best to the inner sovereignty approach that we will be following in this book.

Four Unhelpful Mindsets to Watch Out For

1. Victim Mindset

A victim mindset is characterized by the feeling of being helpless, powerless, and being made the target, or ill-treated and exploited by others. *"Poor me!"* is the constant chant of someone with this mindset.

When you're a victim, the power vests outside of you and with those people. In contrast, when you're a hero, the power vests within you and it helps you tackle the same negative actions of those people in a better way.

2. Martyr Mindset

This mindset pushes people toward being self-sacrificial; their needs always have the lowest priority and they fail to put up boundaries, which allows people to walk all over them.

It is a rather warped form of the Hero Mindset because martyrs are willing to sacrifice it all (including themselves) to help others.

Perhaps there might be some causes for which some people might want to wear a 'martyr mindset'. However, in the arena of career crafting, I don't advocate this mindset. I have found it to be unsustainable and draining —not one that allows us to bring our highest potential into life.

3. Slave Mindset

Just follow orders, execute instructions, and don't question or challenge anything. Keep on working, even if you are burnt out or exhausted, because you think you have no choice. These approaches are typical of embodying a slave mindset at work.

I have often found that many people slip into a slave mindset, just because they are drawing a salary from their employer. They feel obliged to blindly follow orders, get things done without questioning, and not think out-of-the-box. Eventually this kind of mindset actually lands up suffocating and stifling their thinking, creativity, and ironically, their career success too.

4. Baby Mindset

In the baby mindset, people require spoon-feeding and need to be told exactly what they must do at all times. They become highly dependent on whoever offers them this aid.

Another way the baby mindset manifests is that it shows up as an attitude of entitlement—wherein people convince themselves they deserve a raise or a promotion, or anything else they set their eyes upon. It's like a little baby that demands and sulks, *"they were supposed to give this to me",* instead of a mature adult who is willing to co-create that opportunity with their employer through dialogue and effort.

Catch - Question - Switch

You might be wondering why I'm highlighting these four specific mindsets. In my experience as a career coach, I've discovered that these are not only extremely common in the workplace, but also among the most damaging when it comes to career advancement.

So, how do we grow out of these (mostly) limiting and disempowering mindsets? Here, I have a long-term approach as well as a short-term approach for you. And the good news is that the short-term approach is actually the key to implementing and achieving the long-term approach.

Let me explain. The long-term approach is to reprogram our brains so that our default mindset becomes a Hero Mindset instead of a victim, martyr, slave, or baby mindset. However, unconditioning and reconditioning the mind actually happens through practice—*"Neurons that fire together, wire together."* This is where the short-term approach comes in: 'Catch - Question - Switch.'

Every time we catch ourselves operating from one of the four mindsets, we can ask ourselves one of two questions: *"Where is my power?"* or *"Is this helping?"* Based on the answer, we can then switch into a Hero Mindset.

Most of the time, the first question will do the trick and give you the motivation to switch mindsets. When we are in a victim, slave, or baby mindset, our locus of power is always outside of us.

The martyr mindset is more complex, so sometimes you might need the second question to check if the martyr mindset is actually helping you.

It's important to remember that these mindsets are deeply ingrained in most of us, so reaching a stage where we don't slip into them can take time. Even I, with all my years of teaching and practicing the Hero mindset, still find myself slipping into one of the other four mindsets. In fact, if I were to sit down and reflect, I'd probably notice instances of this happening as recently as last week.

The key difference now—and what I invite you to develop as well—is awareness. I used to get stuck in these disempowering mindsets, often staying in them for hours or even days. Now, I've learned to recognize when they occur and consciously shift out of them. I know these mindsets don't serve me, so I choose to shed them, much like a snake shedding its old skin, moving toward something better.

As I've embraced the Hero mindset more and more, I find that the decisions and actions I take from that place serve me far better. And with each positive experience, my resolve to switch mindsets grows even stronger.

I encourage you to try this for yourself. Don't just switch mindsets because I, or any other coach, tells you one is more empowering than another. Experiment with it and see what results you get.

Exercise #3: Practising the Hero Mindset

The aim here is to practice and get comfortable with adopting the Hero mindset. Simultaneously, you must watch out for and practice switching out of the other four disempowering mindsets like the Victim, Martyr, Slave or Baby mindset.

It's time to rely once again on the stopwatch or timer that you used for the data gathering exercise of inner sovereignty. Set it to an hourly interval again.

Every time you hear the beep, do a quick check and see which mindset you currently are in (or might have been in during the past one hour). If it is the Hero Mindset give yourself a pat on the back. If it is one of the other four, then 'catch-question-switch'. If neutral, do nothing.

The more you practice this, and consciously try to adopt a Hero Mindset, you will begin to attune the default tone of your inner chatter to a hero's voice.

And how empowering might that inner voice be as you craft and navigate the ups and downs of your adventurous career journey!

3

Unpacking Success & Personalizing It

"Success is what you envisage it to be. You have to go into any profession knowing what you want because people will place expectations on you and their idea of success could taint yours."

Trey Songz

Who is a successful person, and what does success actually mean?

If you're looking for answers to this question, whether by asking others or browsing online, you might end up thinking that successful people are just like Elon Musk, Bill Gates, or Mukesh Ambani. When we think of success, these names pop up, and the word "success" seems to be almost synonymous with massive wealth, fame, and incredible achievements in one's career.

But let's switch gears for a moment. Picture a young woman working an average job in a bustling city. She's overcome countless challenges from her village life to reach where she is now. Or consider a high-level executive who left a lucrative job to find joy and fulfilment working with an NGO. According to the conventional definition of success, neither of these individuals might see themselves as successful. If they follow the mainstream idea of success, they could feel like they're missing out or falling short.

But here's a thought: they can redefine success in their own way and move closer to feeling successful on their own terms.

45

If you're thinking that the young girl and executive mentioned above are just fictional and that real people do not suffer because of a misguided notion of success, let me share a client's story. This person had left a solid career in finance to start a soul-driven coaching business. She had been doing very well and was really happy with her work. However, she took part in a boot camp for entrepreneurs and came out dejected and broken-hearted. She was extremely upset and came to me with the words, *What am I doing with my life?*

We sat down and started unpacking the layers behind how she was feeling. As she spoke about what had been shared in the bootcamp (strategies for scaling and getting funded), and re-examine it in the light of what was really valuable to her and why she had created her business (autonomy, meaning, and working closely with people) she realized that the mentors' definitions of success didn't match her own - that was all. she actually did not care about either scaling or getting funded.

We're living in a world amidst an ocean of people - who each have categorized success in a certain way or have developed a specific perception of it. Additionally, there are also collective notions of success that are based on your culture, setting, place of living, family values, etc.

And this confusing multiplicity has some very real and significant problems associated with it. It can sabotage our ability to create a wonderful and meaningful career by doing what we enjoy. Worse still, it can lead to the development of chronic feeling of unsuccessfulness. I have personally come across many individuals who, from my paradigm, are doing exceedingly well in their lives. However, they are plagued by nagging thoughts of not being successful. And one of the biggest reasons is that after they do something in pursuit of one definition of success, they step back and evaluate it on the basis of a different definition of success, like my client above.

And even if they themselves do not do so, their spouse, parents, teachers, or friends will end up doing this for them. Either way, they land up feeling unsuccessful.

And so, I ask myself and all of you, why are we subjecting ourselves to this immense confusion and all the problems that it brings along? Why are we constantly judging ourselves on the basis of this subjective label 'success' that has a million interpretations?

You might be thinking now, *"Why not just ditch the label of 'success' altogether to avoid all the confusion and stress it brings?"* I've been there myself. For a while, I tried to completely remove the word 'success' from my life. But here's the thing—I found out that while it sounds nice in theory, it's not very practical in the real world.

Even though I had given up on the label of success, it seemed to follow me everywhere. People throw around the term so frequently that it was impossible for my brain to ignore it. What I eventually realized was that if 'success' is going to be part of my world, I might as well develop a healthier relationship with it. Instead of letting it stress me out, I decided to redefine it in a way that inspires and motivates me.

So, what's in it for you with a refreshed view on success? You'll be able to clearly identify and communicate what success means to you. This clarity will also help you sift through the endless advice and opinions you receive, and focus only on what truly matters. When you realize that some advice comes from a different perspective that doesn't align with yours, you can filter out what doesn't fit your journey. Without such clarity, it's easy to get caught in a loop of chasing milestones that don't resonate with you, leading to self-doubt, dissatisfaction, and less-than-ideal choices, just like in the well-known fable below.

A father and his son are taking their donkey to a nearby village. A group of people along the way share their wisdom and advise them to be more smart in utilizing the resource (i.e. the donkey) that they have. Convinced that the group was right, the son sits on the donkey and they go along till they encounter another group. That group's rather judgmental advice criticizes the young boy for sitting on the donkey while making his old father walk. The father and son switch their positions, and soon enough they are faced with a new group that criticizes the father for choosing the easier way for himself while making his young son walk.

Believing that they needed to act on this advice as well, the father and son both sit on the donkey. Shortly, another group paints them as villains for troubling the poor animal and burdening it with both their weights. Utterly confused now, the father-son duo decides to carry the donkey. A wrong choice, for soon after that, the donkey struggles free and falls into the river beneath.

Much like this unfortunate pair, we too keep taking bits of advice and suggestions from multiple avenues and try to combine it, and end up making a mess of our ideas, plans, and most importantly, our careers.

I am in no way implying that every bit of advice or feedback that comes from outside is misguided. Just that, the advice someone gives you might make perfect sense in the paradigm that they are coming from and yet, it may not work for you because your paradigm, values and goals are different.

But how will you know whether to take someone else's advice or not unless you have first done the inner work of redefining success for yourself?

And that is what we will do in this chapter—in multiple stages. Let's start with the first exercise to explore the associations already existing in our minds on the topic of success.

<u>Exercise #1 - Mind Map of Success</u>

Mind mapping taps into the power of radiant thinking—where ideas spread out like branches from a central concept, connecting to even more ideas. This visual approach captures themes and their many (sometimes surprising) connections automatically.

Because it relies on imagery, it can bypass our inner logical and verbal censor and so we can get insights that we might not get through journaling and other forms of linear writing. Mind mapping is most popularly used for ideating, but I have found that it is also a wonderful way to get a big picture dump onto paper of all the concepts and emotions that our brain uniquely associates with a certain topic—in this case 'success'.

Step 1: Grab a blank sheet of A4 paper. Write 'SUCCESS' boldly in the centre and circle it. This central word will serve as a visual anchor throughout your exercise, reminding your brain that everything written here relates to the theme of success.

Step 2: Gaze at the word 'SUCCESS' and jot down the first five or six associations that come to mind. Don't overthink it; just write whatever pops up. These could be words, emotions, names, or even phrases. The goal is to capture your initial, raw associations without judging or analyzing them.

Step 3: From each initial association, draw three or four lines and add new words or themes related to these prompts.

Use a timer set for 5 minutes to keep this process brisk and intuitive.

This one page now captures your personal mental model of success—what your brain uniquely associates with this concept. There's no right or wrong here; it's simply a reflection of your internal programming.

Take a moment to review your mind map. Are there any surprising elements? Jot down your reflections in your journal. What, if any are the emotions you have associated with success. Are they positive, negative, or mixed? Do you see patterns in how success is linked to processes versus outcomes? Are there particular people or role models highlighted?

Document any insights or reflections that arise as you analyze your map.

The Inner Work of Redefining Success

When you reflect on your mind map of success, you might find it messy and cluttered, sometimes even contradicting itself in places. That's perfectly normal! Cleaning up these inner associations is all part of the journey toward inner sovereignty. Our goal is to redefine success in a way that truly empowers us, creating a definition we can revisit and rely on whenever life's circumstances or outside influences make us question our path. We're on a quest to infuse new meaning into success—one that fits our current stage in life, age, and situation. This refreshed understanding of success can then serve as our guiding compass as we craft our careers and lives.

So, how do we go about creating this personal, sovereign definition of success? First, we need to pause and reflect on how much our thinking has been shaped by societal notions of success. We need to become aware of how culture, social interactions, books, movies, advice, and other influences might have impacted our understanding of what success means to us.

Creating a personalized definition of success that aligns with your values, aspirations, and passions starts with identifying and isolating these influences. Yes, this process might feel a bit overwhelming, and you might wonder if the effort is worth it. But trust me, every minute you invest in this inner decluttering will lead to profound results. The clarity, confidence, and coherence you gain will be invaluable.

Think of your mind as a cluttered room full of thoughts and ideas about success. Just like a deep cleaning for a house, we need to declutter our minds—using a metaphorical flashlight to inspect and decide what to keep and what to toss. You'll likely find four types of mental associations related to success:

1. Associations that are functional and constructive for you, which you can make a conscious choice of retaining

2. Associations that worked well for you at a past stage in life, but which you do not need now for where you would like to go

3. Associations that you realize should never have been there in the first place; the limiting and meaningless ideas that somehow got in, but which can now be weeded out

4. Associations that you already rebelled against, and which shaped your life in a certain way; but now ridding yourself of the rebellion itself will give you the next level of freedom and choice to steer your life in whichever direction you choose

This is a huge inner world task that we are undertaking and so we will journey through it systematically.

Exercise #2: Analysing Success Markers from Past

The goal of this exercise is to become aware of key meanings and markers of success that your mind has inadvertently gathered or concocted over the years. Their sources may be traced back to childhood events, books, movies, people you have met, or experiences you have encountered. Let me give you an example here.

IIT, as a Symbol of Success: When I was young, I lived in an industrial town called Jamshedpur, in an apartment complex where all the balconies faced a common open space in the centre. One morning, I woke up to a loud neighbourhood aunty shouting, *"Congratulations Vikas!"*

I hurried to my balcony and saw all the aunties and uncles cheering and congratulating an older boy. I asked my mother why everyone was so excited, and she explained that he had got IIT. At that moment, I knew I wanted this thing called 'IIT,' even though I was just seven years old and had no clue what it was. It could have been a car, a dress, or even a castle, for all I knew. What mattered was that it seemed like a huge trophy, something that made everyone celebrate you—and I wanted it. I wanted it so badly!

I never once questioned this definition of success I had created in my brain. Nobody else questioned it for me either. The association between IIT and success was deeply entrenched in the collective belief system of the township itself, and so the cultural conditioning only reinforced my personal definition.

As the years progressed I studied diligently through school, took up science and worked hard to get that coveted seat in IIT. I had cut out super-sized alphabets of I,I, and T in big chart paper (almost half my height) and pasted it on my bedroom wall. Every time I thought of my goal of getting into IIT my heart filled with a nice warm glow and raced in excitement. My brain was deeply conditioned with the belief that getting into IIT was the epitome of success.

A point I want to emphasize here is that nobody ever compelled me to burn the midnight oil and study hard. I was always given full freedom by my parents. Never did they, or any teacher or mentor sit me down and tell me that getting into IIT was going to be my measure of success.

Such is the deadly effect of conditioning. It is not direct and intentional. Rather it is so indirect and happens so much at the subconscious level that we don't even realize our brains are getting conditioned. Gaining awareness of the sources of influence (direct or indirect) in your life, and understanding how they have shaped your perception of success is a crucial step in your quest of reclaiming control and crafting a more relevant meaning of the term.

Reflect and journal on the following questions now to explore your early markers of success and examine their relevance to you now:

1. Where did you, or rather your brain, primarily pick up early markers of success in your life?

2. How did these markers influence your choices, decisions, and career trajectory?

3. Are these markers serving your current self well, or do they need re-evaluation?

<u>Exercise #3: Untangling Influence of Close Stakeholders</u>

Start with those closest to you from childhood—your parents or anyone who played a parental role in your life. As children, we often mimic what we see and hear from our parents or other figures of authority, which shapes our behaviors and beliefs. Alternatively, their influence might have taken the opposite direction: their ideas about success may have felt so wrong to you that your life choices were driven by a desire to prove them otherwise. Either way, their impact is significant.

To illustrate this kind of "reverse influence," imagine your father believed success was all about money, but you never agreed. You might have argued with him or silently resented his view. Over time, your desire to disprove his idea of success may have led you to pursue or create a version of success that explicitly excludes money. While you might think you've freed yourself from his notions, you're still being influenced by them. Now, your definition of success is simply the opposite of his—it must exclude money at all costs. Is that really true freedom or choice?

The core of this activity is to reflect on what you believed success meant to these important figures in your life and write it down. But resist the urge to call them up and ask them directly. Here's why: first, their opinions may have evolved over time, no longer reflecting the views they had when they were influencing you. Second, you might have internalized a version of their idea of success that wasn't even what they truly believed. The only version that matters is what you thought they perceived success to be, and how that shaped your own early definition. Beyond parents, you can include a sibling, grandparent, or anyone else who played a major role in your upbringing.

Next, think about your spouse or significant other. They have been deeply connected to you at different life stages, and you are likely to have had some of your most meaningful conversations with them. Over time, it is very likely that your brain might start internalizing their views on success. Again, focus on what you interpreted and understood their idea of success to be—not necessarily what it actually might have been. Write this down, and you may discover new insights into why you think of success the way you do now.

After making notes about each person's beliefs about success, use the reflection questions below to analyze them further. Do this one person at a time, and take your time to understand the impact of each influence on your current mindset.

1. How have his/her notions of success influenced your career and life choices so far?

2. Have you been in blind resistance or rebellion against any of these notions?

3. Which, (if any) of these pointers do you want to retain in your new definition of success?

The first and second questions work to understand how your stakeholders' perceptions of success have indirectly swayed your decisions and shaped your life. Remember to just do this part objectively, as you would analyse a movie script. Please do not fall into a trap of either judging yourself or them for whatever influence you might uncover. The third question is a part of the decluttering mission we have embarked upon, wherein we choose what we want to keep or discard. It is always your choice.

Now, you've understood how you can declutter from past associations, but what can you do about the current stakeholders in your life—people you live with and interact with on a daily basis, who will still continue to project (knowingly or unknowingly) their beliefs of success onto your mind.

Let me tell you about a powerful tool here that I use often and which has truly helped me regain my freedom of choice in such situations and does not let my brain get carried away by the influence of others beliefs. It is called the 'Interesting Point of View'.

The way to set yourself free from the views and opinions that people around you may have and that they may project on you is to merely acknowledge it as an interesting (not good, bad, right, wrong; but merely interesting) point of view and leave it at that. Staying on this path will ensure you do not veer to any of the two extremes that lay on either side- the first being Alignment & Agreement wherein we accept their notions as the absolute truth, or the second being Resistance & Reaction wherein we do not adhere to their notions and rebel to disprove them.

Either of these extremes can trap us in a box, but if we accept their notions as nothing more than an interesting point of view, we are free. In my own life, I never considered academic journal publications to be an important indicator of success but my husband does. Whenever we venture onto this subject and I now hear his thoughts, I internally say to myself that it is an interesting point of view that he has. It has given my brain a peaceful space to live and let live. I don't need to believe his marker is right and therefore make it mine as well. I neither need to rebel against it and prove to him that it is 'wrong'. I can respect his markers of success as his choice AND respect my markers as my choice—appropriate for me.

Exercise #4: Write Your Own Obituary

An obituary is something that celebrates the achievements and accomplishments of one's life upon their demise.

Reflect on any age (be it 90, 100, or even beyond 100) that you would feel content for your life to end at. From that age, treat your obituary as a work of fiction and put down all the elements that you would desire in your actual obituary once you have lived your life up to the age you have chosen. Feel free, optimistic and generous with possibilities as you do this. You have many more years left to learn and gather any new skills to achieve whatever you would like to. So leave aside any limiting thoughts from your current expertise or qualification and just dream idealistically for this exercise.

Write your obituary in the voice of a 3rd person; as if the obituary were written by someone who knew you well.
Here are a few prompts that can guide you in this process:

1. The contributions you hope to make to the world/ your community or profession

2. The values and principles that influenced your life and accomplishments

3. Your significant personal and professional achievements

Don't be fooled by the simplicity or the imaginative nature of this exercise. Many students and participants have got back to me claiming that it is by far one of the most powerful exercises that they have done. So, gift yourself some silent time and uninterrupted space, get a nice hot cup of tea and put your pen to paper.

This exercise works by taking you out of the 'here and now' and giving you a super long term perspective. You get a chance to envision how you want your life and career journey to be looked back upon, and somehow in this process, the things that truly matter to you tend to reveal themselves.

There is absolutely no guarantee that you will live to the age that you have envisioned, but what this activity will do is point towards the direction(s) that will feel most satisfying for you to walk in—which you can now choose to include in your new personalized definition of success.

Exercise #5: Value Clarification Prompts

Why is this essential for redefining success? Think of your personal values as your internal compass—they guide you toward what genuinely matters to you. If you create a definition of success that doesn't align with those values, you'll feel like you're constantly swimming against the tide. This leads to what I call a "non-coherent existence," where, despite reaching your milestones, you end up feeling unfulfilled or find that satisfaction is fleeting.

I've seen this repeatedly in my coaching practice and research and I know it from my own experience as well. High achievers who reach their goals only to wonder why it doesn't feel as rewarding as they'd hoped. It often comes down to a misalignment with their values. But the moment we bring our definition of success into harmony with what we truly care about, everything shifts. The journey itself becomes more meaningful, _and_ the accomplishments feel much more satisfying. Journal with these prompts to help you identify your personal values.

1. Childhood Reflection: The moments that you felt most fulfilled and the underlying values in these moments.

2. Role Models: Who do you admire, and which of their values resonate with you? Why?

3. Decision Making: The factors that you prioritized while making any difficult decisions and the values that these factors reflect.

4. Non-Negotiables: The things that you would never compromise upon. Why?

5. Discontentment & Discomfort: Moments when you felt most upset or frustrated, and which values were challenged in them.

Exercise #6: Redefining Success for Yourself

We now come to the final stage, the creation of a new definition of success. I cannot overemphasize the importance of aligning this new definition with the personal values you've just uncovered. A simple version of your new definition of success might simply list those values, and that's a solid start. But don't hesitate to expand— add more dimensions, specifics, or even enablers that bring those values to action in your life. Revisit your notes from all the previous exercises in this chapter as you do this.

There's no universal rule for what you should include as your markers of success. This is entirely personal, and you have the freedom to craft a definition that resonates with you, in any format you prefer. Some people find clarity in a single sentence, while others write a more detailed paragraph. Bullet points are also an effective way to capture key elements, and in fact, that's the approach I've taken in my own definition of success, which I'm sharing with you as an example below.

My current definition /markers of success:
- Expressing & sharing my philosophy and art
- Facilitating human potential and consciousness
- Embodying Love, Light, & Beauty
- Supporting loved ones (people & causes)
- Communing with inner & outer nature

Always remember that the primary audience and consumer of your personal definition of success is only *you*. So once you write it down, you can do an intuitive test by reading it aloud to yourself and see how it makes you *feel*.

1. Does this new definition of success feel expansive to you?
2. Does it motivate you to jump out of bed and start working with enthusiasm and vigour?
3. Does it make you feel like channelling all your life force energy into action?

Keep redrafting, rewording and playing with your new personalized definition of success till you reach a stage where what you have written really really lights you up.

My one suggestion, however, would be to use words that describe directions rather than precise destinations. Examples of direction are the inclusion of values like knowledge, love, health, wealth or abundance. Examples of destination would mean putting down a specific academic degree, partner, body metrics, bank balance etc. alongside these values. If you put in a specific amount that you want to earn, or a specific milestone you want to reach, it runs the risk of limiting you, and secondly it can also leave you with a sense of void once you achieve it.

We will visit these points once again in the chapter where we talk about setting goals and visions. And at that time I will guide you on what precautions you can take when including specific measurable outcomes into your goals and visions. Because there are benefits to creating precise (outcome based visions), and we will explore how to do that mindfully. However, we have much, much inner work to go before we get to playing with the tricky, double-edged, uber-powerful tool of goals.

So for now, let's approach success not as an end goals but as a directions. And later (after chapter 10), we can set specific goals that will be aligned with these success directions.

Exercise #7: Pod Discussions

Discuss what you have uncovered as well as your experience of doing the exercises with your Pod. Please take turns to read out your obituary (in the third person). This can be a very powerful experience.

At the very end, share the redefined version of success that you have now crafted for yourself. Elaborate on the values that you have chosen as the foundation for your life and career, and what these values stand for in your mind. Owning this in front of others will help you own it better for yourself.

Exercise #8: Reinforcing Your New Definition of Success

Redefining success is just the first step; to truly benefit from it, you need to make it a core part of your mental model. Since repetition is key to updating our inner world, write down your new definition of success and your values. Place it somewhere visible—on your desk, pinboard, or wherever you'll see it often. Your subconscious mind will gradually absorb these new ideas, and over time, they'll become its default association with success. You can also create short verbal reminders based on your new definition and repeat them to yourself.

The next step is to begin integrating it into your daily life and decisions. Use your hourly timer again and each time it beeps ask yourself: *"If I were someone who values X, Y, and Z (based on your chosen values) and saw success as _____, what would I do in this moment? What would I say yes to? What actions would I take?"* By doing this consistently, you'll begin to get into a habit of actually living in alignment with your new parameters of success.

An added benefit of creating your own personalized definition of success is that since it is unique and personal to you, your mind will soon stop comparing your journey (in unhealthily competitive ways) with that of others. You will realize that each person is on their very own 'success journey', and that you are not all on the same race track, headed toward the same finish line. It's like each person is blossoming and growing along their own unique success paths. As this realization grows stronger, feelings like jealousy and envy will quite naturally fall away from your experience and you will actually be able to cheer and support others wholeheartedly in their success missions as well—authentically and from your heart .

4

De-Villainizing and Redefining Work

"Always you have been told that work is a curse and labour a misfortune. But I say to you that when you work you fulfil a part of earth's furthest dream, assigned to you when the dream was born, and in keeping yourself with labour you are in truth loving life, and to love life through labour is to be intimate with life's inmost secret."

Kahlil Gibran

How many times have you said, 'I'm going to work'? Probably more than you can count. And let's be honest—unless you're one of the lucky few who've never felt a twinge of negativity about work, that statement might come with a side of resignation, stress, or even a little anxiety. Those lucky few, though, might say it with a sense of gratitude, happiness, and maybe even excitement.

I want to facilitate more people to join that lucky group. My goal is to help you shake off the unpleasant connotations that have unfairly stuck to the idea of 'work' in your mind. I want to empower you to see it from a new perspective, one from where you can craft a fulfilling and meaningful experience in your professional life.

Remember the self-fulfilling prophecy we talked about in Chapter 1? If we expect work to be a chore, a burden, or a source of stress, we're setting ourselves up to experience exactly that. It's like we're writing the script for our own dissatisfaction.

I've made it my personal mission to de-villainize work—to help people see that it's not the monster we've made it out to be. And I say 'we' because I've been there too. There was a time when I thought work was the biggest problem in my life. Just thinking about it or dragging myself into the office used to make me feel hollow and helpless.

As I shared in the introduction, my journey to understand the person-work relationship started because of how much work was affecting me—and not in a good way. But I decided to change that, to reinvent my relationship with work, and now I'm inviting you to join me on a similar journey. Just as I've seen the incredible benefits of transforming my experience with work, I'm confident you will too.

Comparing 'Work' to 'Sports'

You might be raising an eyebrow at the title of this section, wondering where on earth I'm going with this. Work and sports? They seem like two completely different worlds, right? What could possibly be gained from comparing them?

Well, stick with me for a bit—you might be surprised by where this exercise takes you.

First, let's get clear on what I mean by 'sports.' We know by now that a single word can trigger a whole range of ideas, depending on how our brains interpret it. So, when I say 'sports,' I'm talking about anything that comes to mind for you. It could be indoor or outdoor sports, something you do for fun, for competition, or even as a profession. It might involve a team or be something you do solo. And as for 'work,' I'm pretty sure you've already got a good idea of what that includes.

Now, grab a pen and paper, and let's do a quick exercise. Draw two columns on the sheet. In the first column, jot down all the similarities you can think of between work and sports. At first, this might seem tricky—our minds are so used to seeing them as completely separate activities. But give it a little time and thought. In my workshops, I've seen groups come up with as many as fifty similarities! I'm challenging you to aim for at least twenty. Once you've done that, move to the second column and list all the differences you can think of.

Now, let's circle back to List 1—the similarities. If I had to guess, your list might include things like teamwork, performance, success, failure, wins, losses, growth, skill, and maybe even stress, fatigue, or fear of failure. And I hope you've got a lot more on that list too! Don't stop there—dig deeper and add more nuanced aspects like coaching, mentoring, leadership, and achievement. Think about even those elements that can sometimes, but not always, show up in both work and sports, and keep adding them to your list.

Now, about List 2—the differences. I want you to look at each point you've written and ask yourself, "Is this a necessary difference?" For many of them, you might start to realize that the differences are more about perception than reality. They're distinctions we've created based on the mental models we have about what work and sports are supposed to be. If you find a difference that doesn't feel necessary anymore, go ahead and strike it off the list.

You might be wondering why I'm encouraging you to make a long list of similarities and shorten the list of differences. Here's the thing—'work' and 'sports' are just labels, much like the label of 'success' we explored in Chapter 3. I want to challenge your brain to uncover why one of these labels tends to carry a much heavier, more prejudiced load than the other.

When we think of sports, most of us light up. We associate it with excitement, energy, and positive vibes. We want to jump in, even if there's no tangible reward involved. But when it comes to work, our attitude often shifts, and not always in a good way.

Let me share a personal story to bring this home. When I first joined IIM Bangalore as an assistant professor, I was teaching subjects that I genuinely loved. Work became my sanctuary, and teaching brought me immense joy and satisfaction. At the same time, I'd play basketball in the evenings on campus—a sport I'd loved for years. But here's the thing: my basketball skills and stamina weren't what they used to be, and trying to play with much younger, faster players (typically the MBA students on campus) wasn't exactly a recipe for fun.

So, there I was—having an amazing time at work, but not really enjoying my time on the court. And yet, I noticed something odd about how I talked about these two activities. Every morning, I'd say, "I'm going to work," in a tone that didn't match the pleasure I actually got from my job. On the flip side, my voice would perk up when I mentioned going to play, even though the reality was far less satisfying. My experience and the stories I told myself about these activities were out of sync. And once I caught that, I got curious— really curious—about why that was.

Inner Possibilities with Work

I figured the best place to begin was to look at research related to the inner world experiences associated with both 'work' and 'sports'. I soon realized that I wasn't the first to ask these questions. I was following in the footsteps of some pretty brilliant minds, none more influential than Mihaly Csikszentmihalyi and his groundbreaking work on the concept of 'flow.'

In simple terms, flow is that mental state where you're so fully engaged, immersed, and energized by what you're doing that everything else just fades away. You're in the zone, excelling at the task, and contributing positively to your own life or even the lives of others. It's a state where peak performance feels almost effortless. Who wouldn't want to experience that, right?

What I learnt is that a few things make it easier to achieve flow in any activity: having a structured task with clear goals, ensuring there's room for feedback, and balancing the challenge level to match your skills. Csikszentmihalyi had also studied the differences between active leisure and passive leisure, and found that the former is much more conducive to entering a state of flow. As I dived deeper into his research, I started connecting these dots back to my earlier comparison of 'work' and 'sports.'

Think about sports for a moment—something Csikszentmihalyi would classify as active leisure. It checks all the boxes needed for flow: structure, challenge, feedback, and clear goals. Now, consider work—surprisingly, it also meets those same criteria. But what about passive leisure, like sitting around, chatting with friends, or binge-watching shows? Those activities, while relaxing, don't offer the same potential for flow. They lack the structure and challenge needed to truly engage your mind. They're great for unwinding, but they don't provide that deep sense of fulfilment.

This idea resonated with me because I'd often found passive leisure to be less enjoyable than I expected. I'd go to parties or social gatherings, only to come home feeling bored, drained, or even a bit sad instead of recharged. The same thing had also happened on vacations that didn't include any active leisure—making me wonder if something was innately wrong with me!

These personal experiences gave me an important clue. But the real aha moment came when I stumbled upon something else Csikszentmihalyi had studied—something psychiatrists have documented as well: Sunday Neurosis. Sundays had always been challenging for me, especially during the tougher phases of my life. It turns out I wasn't alone. The term 'Sunday Neurosis' was coined by psychologists and therapists who noticed a spike in calls from people needing help on this particular day of the week. Sunday, supposedly a day for rest and relaxation, can actually be one of the most distressing days for many.

Why is that? Well, if we imagine a spectrum of our mental states, flow sits at one end—a state of high productivity, focus, and alignment. At the other end is something called 'psychic entropy,' the chaotic opposite of flow. When we're in flow, we're completely absorbed in what we're doing. We're focused, our inner world is coherent, and everything feels aligned. It's like being in a meditative state, but with a task at the center.

On the flip side, psychic entropy is when our minds are scattered, disorganized, and all over the place. This is what often happens on Sundays when there's no structured plan for the day. Without that structure, we're more vulnerable to falling into psychic entropy, which can make us feel like we're losing control over our inner world.

Learning all this made me realize just how unfairly we've been treating 'work.' We've painted it as the villain in our well-being story, when in fact, it has the potential to do us a great service. Work can actually be a powerful tool for maintaining our mental sanity. One day without work can disrupt our mental health, yet we rarely see work for the blessing it can be. Beyond just providing us with a paycheck, work can be a means of self-expression, creativity, productivity, and even social connection. When managed properly, work can be an antidote to psychic entropy, a safeguard against feelings of madness, depression, worthlessness, and meaninglessness.

Having personally experienced all these states and emotions in the past, I've developed a deep respect and gratitude for anything that can help combat them. And I was extremely delighted to note that 'work' could be that saviour and blessing - not just in my life, but all our lives!

How Work was Villainized

Like a hero (remember, that we all are heroes and follow the hero's journey in specific stages of our life), I embarked on a mission to vindicate 'work' from the defamation it has endured and restore its reputation.

Exploring our cultural heritage and revisiting the historical perspective of work in Indian culture, I found a timeless wisdom: work was considered worship. But, like in many other aspects of our lives today, our approach towards work got conditioned by other influences. For example, during the Roman era there was a definitive disrespect and disregard for work in certain parts of Europe. The narrative was centered around a premise that human beings inherently did not want to work. There was a certain judgment associated with people who worked, and the 'working classes' were believed to be socially inferior to the 'elite classes' who never worked.

Over time, this narrative gained traction, and 'work' began to get negative connotations associated with it. This new meaning of work got infused into movies, literature, music and art. Eventually, this approach towards 'work' began to get reinforced more and more and before we knew it 'work' became the bad guy for most of us.

Just look at the general narratives around work-life balance that we, as a society, have built today. The widely accepted structure of a five-day work week after which we can 'enjoy weekends' makes it feel like those five days are a painful time that we must endure and simply get through, so as to reap the benefits that work-free weekends bring. Does it mean that one cannot enjoy their life while working? It is very easy to draw this conclusion from the things we see, hear, and experience around us today. But take it from someone who has been through these same feelings, and now finds the greatest enjoyment in her work, that this is yet another aspect of the unfair villainization of work. And in my opinion, this model has to change.

I, and a few others like me, have challenged this model and discarded it from our minds - and I invite you to do the same! Now, don't get me wrong—I'm not saying you need to work all the time, just as you wouldn't want to party or play all the time. You can still cherish your weekends as "work-free time," but do it from a place of balance and variety, not from a mindset that sees work as a necessary burden to escape.

Pushing Against the Tide

When I realized that work can be our greatest friend as well as our worst enemy I made it my life's mission to help others de-villainize work in their minds. I realized that because of the self-fulfilling prophecy of our own belief systems, as long as people believed that work was something that is stressful, draining, boring or a burden— that indeed is the work experience they would create for themselves. I had myself been there and done that, and that is a 'real' way of experiencing one's work as well.

So when I started teaching my career crafting courses and workshops, I used to start with a discussion about how work can be a gift and blessing in our lives. However, I realized that I was pushing against the tide here. The opposite conditioning in society - of work being a burden or annoyance or necessary evil was just way too strong. Soon, I realized that it was no longer just a benign historical perspective that I was trying to reverse. I was up against some powerful brainwashing that was happening in real time, every day. And this was the strong force of the tide that I had to pull my students thinking beyond.

So who or what, you might ask, is perpetuating these harmful and toxic beliefs about work in our society today. Ironically, it's the 'Leisure Industry'. Vacations and leisure activities are often marketed as a *"much-needed escape from the pressures of work."* It's a clever marketing ploy designed to boost sales, but it also reinforces the notion that work is always stressful and something to be forcefully endured—the *grind* as they put it. These advertisements paint work as an unwelcome necessity, and while I have no issue with the leisure industry per se, their narrative sustains (and even further fuels) the already dysfunctional mental models about work.

Think about it: what is 'work' really, other than a label we've created? We put ourselves through unnecessary stress and tension over something we've invented. If we could change our mental model and choose a different meaning for this concept, we could open up our brain (and through that our lives) to experience radically new possibilities in our work.

You have the power to redefine work in a way that you want to experience it. It can be as exhilarating as an adventure sport, as calming as meditation, as fun and interactive as a party, or as soulfully expressive as art or music. The possibilities are endless - and you get to choose!

But before you can embrace this new reality, you need to craft a new meaning of work for yourself—just as you did with success. It's up to you to create a definition of work that is free from the negativity that culture has saddled it with, and aligned with how you truly want to experience it. This new meaning should be the one you think of whenever you hear the term 'work.'

Redefining Work

Just like redefining success, redefining work is a crucial step on our inner work journey and a key component in achieving inner sovereignty as we craft our careers.

We first need to understand what we're dealing with—what's currently shaping our perception of work—so we can decide what to change and what to keep. The initial step is to gain clarity on what your mind has absorbed about the concept of work from the countless external influences it has encountered over time, and therefore what it currently associates with work.

Exercise #1: Mind Map of Work

This exercise is the first out of different stages of inner work that we will do on this topic. On a piece of paper, put down the word 'work' and create a mental map of all the emotions, thoughts, ideas, and associations by listing down whatever comes to your mind related to the word. Then, go a step ahead and list down what you associate with each of the preliminary associations that you made with work (just like you had done when you made your mind map on success).

The goal of this exercise is simply to engage in a non-judgmental exploration of what is currently in your mind. Once your map is complete, look at all the associations and sub-associations you have listed down, identify which are the functional associations that you want to keep and which are the ones that you would no longer want to keep in your mental model of work. While you could not exert control over letting them into your brain (for they often slip in, unnoticed, from the many influences around us), you can definitely choose whether they should remain there or not, going forward.

Exercise #2: Reverse Engineering the Flow State

There are numerous benefits that can come with work; it can be an opportunity to create and build, to express oneself, to showcase strengths, to improve the lives of others, to connect with others, to grow & learn, and more. And the best part? Since you are customizing a new meaning of 'work' for yourself, you can pick and choose whatever shape you wish for your work to take, whatever outcomes you hope to gain from it, and change its meaning to align with your expectations.

However, there are two approaches to looking at work that will make a worthy addition to everyone's definition. The first is to look at work as an opportunity to achieve the state of flow. The second is to look at it as an opportunity for learning. The link between work and learning comes more easily to us and it is more acceptable to our minds; so I'm certain that a lot of you will continue to see work as an opportunity to learn.

But with respect to flow, I have met a lot of people who believe that flow is something that 'just happens'. They undoubtedly feel it, experience its power, even enjoy the invigoration that it brings with it, but do not give it further thought. They accept flow as simply a stroke of luck that comes to them when they are engaged in certain activities.

They fail to ask themselves two very important questions. Firstly, can the state of flow be achieved through work? And secondly, can there be things deliberately done to increase the chances of achieving flow at work? The answer to both these questions is an emphatic yes!

For the purpose of this exercise, recollect some of the times in the past when you have experienced flow. These could be work-related, leisure-related, or from any other aspect of your life too.

Try to remember that time in as much detail as possible, and note down exactly what you were doing, where you were, and how you felt in the state of flow. Try to recollect around for or five such instances and now using this data, reflect on the following questions:

1. Were there any common elements in these experiences (type of task, time of day, environment, etc.)

2. Were there any routines or habits that you followed before experiencing flow? (Specific habits can work as cues for your brain to direct it towards a state of flow)

3. Were there any specific mindset or attitudes that helped you find your flow?

At the end of your exploration of these questions, you have created a first draft of a personalized flow profile. For example, my first draft of a personalized flow profile included elements like working in outdoor or natural settings, typically working alone, activities that involve some kind of self expression (art, writing, speaking etc), and activities that involve some form of design and creation (be it flower arrangements or workshop designing).

Once you have done this, you're in a better position to try to reverse engineer experiences of flow for yourself. Knowing what factors, actions, environments, and mindsets are conducive to you attaining flow, you can try to recreate and tweak these elements in any scenario (including work) and give yourself the best shot at achieving the flow state.

There is yet another later of fine-tuning that you can do to the personalized flow profile that you have created by incorporating into it certain elements that seem to have a universal impact on most people with regard to experiencing flow.

Csikszentmihalyi has identified eight common characteristics of flow through his research and i have found that these can also be used to reverse engineer a flow state for ourselves. Even in tasks where otherwise, the chances of achieving flow might be lower. The eight characteristics are:

1. Clear goals
2. Immediate (unambiguous) feedback
3. Balance between skills and challenges
4. Deepened concentration
5. Present is what matters
6. Control is no problem
7. Altered sense of time
8. Loss of ego

I've successfully managed to reverse engineer flow experiences for myself using some of these points as clues, and I encourage you to try the same. Just experiment with them in different tasks and see which ones click for you. You don't need all eight. Working with just a few is enough most of the time.

The first five points are especially easy to incorporate into almost any task or project. You can set clear goals for yourself and build in regular feedback loops to keep track of your progress. You can also adjust the difficulty level in your work so that you challenge yourself just a bit beyond your current skill level—too much of a stretch can create anxiety, while too little can lead to boredom. Then you can carve out uninterrupted blocks of time in your workday to focus and concentrate deeply, free from distractions. And while you're at it, you can also practice mindfulness to keep your attention anchored in the present moment and on the task at hand.

But here's the thing: don't become overly focused on pursuing flow itself. The aim is to increase your chances of experiencing it during your work, not to turn it into an obsession. I would recommend thinking of flow more as a desirable byproduct of engaging intimately with your work, and not an end goal in itself. Remember, flow isn't always necessarily beneficial to you or others. Even activities like video games, which can have their own set of problematic outcomes, can induce a flow state and become addictive.

In Csikszentmihalyi's own words, flow is *"a state in which people are so involved in an activity that nothing else seems to matter; the experience is so enjoyable that people will continue to do it even at great cost, for the sheer sake of doing it".*

Exercise #3: Your Desired ROTI from Work

ROTI, or Return on Time Invested, is about identifying what you want to gain from the time, energy, and attention you pour into your work. Most of us tend to equate these returns solely with money—work hard, earn a paycheck, end of story. But that thinking is so limiting! There's a treasure trove of benefits beyond just a salary: the knowledge you acquire, the experiences you savor, the connections you build, the boost to your self-esteem, opportunities for creativity, expression, contribution, recognition and so much more. And now that you know about the flow state, why not include that into your ROTI list as well?

Be bold while creating these new expectations; include everything that you desire in the current state of your life and see if you can transform work into an opportunity to experience that. Give your work a chance to become a channel of true joy, contentment, and satisfaction in your life. Do not censor it and do not try to justify to anyone why you want what you want. This is your list - and your authentic heart's desire at this stage in your life.

As you make this list, do note that your ROTI list will change/grow as you change and evolve through life. When I made my first ROTI@work list about 15 years back, it included things like, an opportunity for self expression, a chance to experience flow, an occasion to learn, space to channel my creativity, and personal development. With the passing of years, these have become a 'given' in any project I now do. Today, my ROTI list includes more ambitious asks— interacting with people who are interesting and energizing, transforming peoples realities with work, spending time in nature, and embodying love and light.

Your list too, will keep evolving, making work an increasingly richer invitation to more and more wonderful possibilities with each passing year.

Exercise #4: Creating a New Definition of Work

With all the insights you've gathered from the earlier exercises, it's now time to redefine what work means to you. While others may continue to see work as a necessary evil, you have the power to reshape it into something meaningful and fulfilling.

Your new definition can be as brief as a few sentences or as detailed as a paragraph—it's entirely up to you. What matters most is that it feels positive, encouraging, and aligns with your goals and the outcomes you wish to achieve. This new definition should be something you hold dear in your mind and heart, something you turn to whenever you think or talk about work.

It is also important to do a quick alignment check here to see whether your new definitions of work and success and your personal values are all in coherence. This does not mean that you have to repeat the exact same set of aspects in both the definitions and in your values list. It simply means that they should not all be pulling you in opposite directions. Ensure that your new definition of work does not contain any elements that contradict your personal values, because work will never feel rewarding for you if such is the case. And after all, isn't that what all this inner work has been about—making work feel truly fulfilling?

Exercise #5: Pod Discussions

Similar to the process that we have followed previously, you are encouraged to discuss the inner work about 'work' with your Pod members. Do share your insights of your mind map, as well as the factors you have identified to boost your chances of experiencing flow at work.

Definitely read out your unique ROTI@work list. This is your BOLD ASK to the universe and to yourself. Be proud of it and own it.

Once every member has shared their personal experiences with the exercise thus far, share your new definitions of work. Explain why you have crafted it in that particular way, and how it aligns with your new notion of success and your inherent personal values. Talking aloud about this new meaning adds a layer of finality and truth to it, something that will help you immensely in internalizing it for yourself as well.

Exercise #6: Reinforcing your New Definition of Work

Changing years of conditioning doesn't happen overnight. It's one thing to create a new definition of work, but it's another to weave it into the fabric of your daily life. We must try to make it a part of our everyday approach and assimilate it deeply into our mental models so that whenever we hear or think about the term 'work', this new meaning takes the centre stage in our brain.

Start by harnessing the power of repetition. Write down your new definition and display it somewhere you'll see it often—on your desk, in your home office, or on a bulletin board. Then, use an alarm on your phone or stopwatch to check in with yourself at random moments. When you're about to dive into a task, pause and ask yourself: "How would I approach this if I truly embraced my new definition of work?" Apply this mindset to everything you do, whether it's a task you love, a chore you'd rather skip, or anything in between. The more you practice, the more deeply this new meaning will take root.

Eventually hearing the term 'work' will invoke the new meaning of work that you have chosen for yourself. Instead of relying on the age-old and unfairly painted picture of work, you now have an empowering and exciting mental model of work in your mind. Couple this refreshingly new perspective that you have on work with the new perspective that you have of success, and you have the most powerful duo in your hands (or rather, in your mind) to craft for yourself a career of your dreams

5

Integrating Money, Work & Service

"The world is full of abundance and opportunity, but far too many people come to the fountain of life with a sieve instead of a tank car, a teaspoon instead of a steam shovel. They expect little and as a result they get little."

Ben Sweetland

Let's talk about one of civilization's most judged inventions - Money!

An abstract concept constructed by human beings, but which has now become the leading driver behind most actions.

A label that we widely use, but have never really stopped to think about and deeply understand.

A subject of conversation that we often try to hide away from, and yet one that, as a society, we cannot stop idolizing.

I had already been working toward helping people craft meaningful career experiences for a decade, before I realized that something was missing in my inner work curriculum. The missing subject was money!

How did this happen?
It happened (as it often does) when I experienced some turbulence in my own relationship with money and work. It served as an eye-

opener that many others were perhaps struggling as I was, and I realized how important the construct of money can be in our overall career-crafting experience.

When I was a salaried employee at IIM Bangalore, my work and my service had my undivided focus. The money just automatically came into my bank account, and I never had to think or worry about it.

The 'jolt'—going back to the Hero's Journey, the jolt is the call to action that makes us step out of our comfort zone and do what is required of us at the stage of life we're in—came for me when I transitioned from being a salaried employee and ventured into freelancing and entrepreneurship. Suddenly, I had to start thinking about how money correlated with the work that I was doing. And it proved to be quite difficult.

Similar to the usual trajectory that follows a jolt, I met a mentor (in my case, I actively sought coaching) who helped me redefine money in my inner world and give it a legitimate and joyful place in my business and in my heart.

I realized that over the years I had accumulated quite a lot of limiting, negative, and unfavourable notions about money. Although I had already embarked on a parallel journey to start healing my relationship with money, that had been more from the perspective of my personal life (money EQ^2). But in my professional life, I had never stopped to think about the delicate strings that connect money, work, and service and this was what my coach helped me untangle.

---

[2] You can access a 2 hour masterclass on this topic at:
https://craftingourlives.com/book-resouces/

Decoding our Relationship with Money

Our relationship with money is highly personal, as well as complex and each of us will have very unique and distinct feelings about it. If you think about it, it is rather ironic that all these labels created by humans themselves, like 'success', 'work', or 'money', are now almost dictating the human experience. We generally operate with a fixed set of ideals and beliefs about these labels; unless, of course, you have already embarked on a journey of inner work and redefined the concepts for yourself.

The fixed set of beliefs about money that our brains have been conditioned with over time leads to most of us carrying some kind of baggage about it; you can think of them as 'money wounds'. These wounds are often inflicted upon us in our childhood, and get progressively deeper due to the things we see and experience thanks to our brains' self-fulfilling prophecy.

Irrespective of whether you are running your own business or are a salaried employee, it is essential to heal your money wounds, and in a broader sense, heal your very relationship with money. And you can go a step further, like we have done with success and work, to ask yourself what you want your reality with money to be and mould this manmade construct of 'money' to be whatever you want it to be.

Let's do a quick spot check here. Think of three significant people in your life whose actions and perceptions are likely to have influenced your reality with money. These could be your parents, siblings, or any other close stakeholder in your life. Once you have three people in your mind, ask yourself whether they all related to money in the same way. You will soon understand that even within this narrow category of three people that you have chosen, multiple unique realities of money exist.

Why then can we not create our own unique reality of money —one that aligns with how we want to think about this label and how we want to relate with it?

This is the very question I asked myself as I embarked on the journey to heal my relationship with money.

At one point in my life I used to be so disconnected from money that I did not even handle my own money. I used to think of money as 'dull', and even 'dirty', and pretended to have nothing to do with it. I literally looked down upon people who were 'money-minded'. A personal disruption in my life however forced me to start managing and handling my own finances, and I was thrown into deep waters. I was super uncomfortable, but eventually learnt that the problem was not with money but with the way I thought about it. The more I thought about it as being dirty, lowly, or evil, the worse my ability to receive, manage and handle it adeptly.

During the process of healing my own relationship with money, I discovered that I actually had many fears about money too. Spending or carrying large sums of money, or making any big transactions would make me really nervous. Because I was aware of the workings of the human brain, I could make the correlation that my fear while handling money indicated that my reptilian brain (which you will learn more about in Chapter 6) was getting activated. Now, this is not the smartest or sharpest part of our brain, which meant that I wasn't making the best decisions with my money or handling it in the wisest way. And this is why I wanted to heal it.

Speaking from my own journey, I am here to tell you that it is completely possible to start changing your relationship with money and make it an enriching and meaningful entity in your life. It is, no doubt, a slow and layered process, but it is definitely worth it.

My relationship with money today is much more relaxed and joyful as compared to where I started from. However it can still be better because inner work is an ongoing journey. And just like you, I too am on the path to make my reality with money more abundant, secure, and expansive.

Exercise #1: Choosing a New Relationship with Money

So once again we will use the simple but highly effective tool of mind mapping. Put down the word 'money' on a sheet of paper and candidly list down all the associations, emotions, and beliefs that your mind makes. I urge you not to censor your thoughts for this task; don't be judgemental or overthink, simply put down whatever comes to your mind.

Once you've got a nice jumble of thoughts on paper, it's time to categorize them. What associations and beliefs do you want to hold on to? Which ones need a little tweaking? And which ones are just dead weight, dragging you down and ready to be tossed out? As you're sorting through, make sure these choices align with your vision of what you want your new relationship with money to be. And don't forget—this should also resonate with your redefined ideas of success and work (from chapters 3 and 4). If these three concepts—money, success, and work—aren't working in harmony, you'll feel like you're constantly being pulled in opposite directions.

The big goal here? We're aiming to rewire your brain's entire approach to money, shifting from whatever old habits and hang-ups you've got to a new, healthier, and more empowered mindset.

Now, here's an interesting little tidbit: when it comes to healing any relationship—be it with a parent, a spouse, a friend, or anyone else—both sides usually need to put in the work. Whether that's through changing behaviors, attending therapy, or following a counselor's advice, it's a two-way street. But here's the good news for you: money is a completely neutral party in your relationship with it. It doesn't come with its own baggage, conditioning, or history. In fact, it's just sitting there, waiting for you to decide how you want to relate to it.

You're in the driver's seat. You get to decide whether your relationship with money is full of stress and judgment, or if it's one of positivity and empowerment. It's a one-person job, and the keys to this transformation are completely in your hands.

Money and Service: A Powerful Partnership

There is a beautiful and intricate symbiotic relationship between 'money' and the 'service' that we provide which I have come to understand and appreciate only within the last three or four years. In hindsight, it seems like common sense; something that I should have seen right at the start, but at the time, it did not seem so obvious.

Back then, I harboured the illusion that service should be just about giving to people, and that I should not ask or expect money in return. This was all a result of my past conditioning and operating from this place used to make me oscillate between two unhelpful extremes: feeling noble, virtuous, and superior, and then swinging to the other end of being tired, burnt out, and drained. Uncovering the interdependent relationship between money and service has helped me experience a sustainable flow of energy, motivation and peace in the work I do. It has literally been a game changer in my career.

One of the 'mantras' that helped me along this journey, which was given to me by one of my mentors, is *'I Serve; I Deserve'*. Even just reading it, you might feel its power.

Many of us (and yes, I was right there with you) struggle with the idea that we're worthy of abundance. We carry deep-seated beliefs about money, often rooted in the idea that receiving it is wrong or that asking for it diminishes the value of our service. It's like we all have an inherent challenge with receiving. But that mantra—*"I Serve; I Deserve"*—started to unravel such knots for me, especially in the context of my work.

I started telling myself, *"I serve people, and therefore, I deserve to be compensated and nurtured."* I repeatedly told myself that it was okay to receive.

Money empowers us to take care of ourselves and our loved ones, to keep our bodies and minds healthy, and even to improve the way we serve others, or the number of people we can serve. And here's the key—these two things always grow in tandem. If you're serving more people or providing more value, then you get compensated more. Once you embrace this truth, abundance has a way of finding you.

And let's talk about what you can do with that abundance. Whether it's creating a more comfortable home, a better office, hiring house help to lighten your load, or growing a team to expand your business—money opens up a world of possibilities.

Money is also a powerful tool for personal growth, which I believe is one of the most worthwhile uses of it, as the returns are transformative. You can use money to hire mentors or coaches who help you navigate your inner world challenges, or enroll in courses that enhance your skills and growth. These are the some of the things I began to gift myself once I made peace with receiving more.

And looking back, I see them not just as indulgences, but as wise investments in both myself and my business. Because, as I grew, my business grew with me. In fact, I can say with total confidence that these investments are why I'm now able to share 'career alchemy' and all the wisdom I've gathered with you today.

<u>Exercise #2: Embracing Money-Service Synergy</u>

Step 1: Pick a hypothetical project that is related to any form of service (contributing to the betterment or wellbeing of other people or worthy causes). And it is imperative here not to obsess over which project to pick. The specifics of the project do not matter at this stage, and that is the beauty of inner work—undertaking it for one project will unlock benefits for all other projects that you will do in the future. The main purpose is to create a context where your fears, limiting beliefs, and any unfavorable conditioning related to mixing money and service can emerge to be addressed.

Step 2: Now, look to identify any role model (choose someone on whom you can easily gather information) who is doing any work that you believe is impactful, or which serves and helps other people, and which has a purpose. The person you pick need not be in the same line of work as you, but if they are in a related field it makes the subsequent steps of this exercise easier for your brain - so look for such a person if possible. An additional requirement for the person you choose is that they must be doing such work as a business, and gaining revenue from it.

Research as much as you can about this person and the business—what motivated them, how they set it up, what challenges they faced, etc. Through this research, you will feed your brain new possibilities. Our brains have typically developed a lot of models (from various influences around us) wherein people run charities, or engage in socially contributive work without earning money in return. It is necessary, however, to also create some new models for your brain that go contrary to its prior conditioning and expose it to a possibility where meaningful work can be rewarded with money.

Step 3: Circle back to the original cause & project that you had picked and redesign it in a way that includes abundant money inflow alongside the service outflow. You can be playful and creative in this redesign. We are just playing with possibilities here. You don't have to ever execute this project!

Step 4: Take an imaginative leap into the future to a time (how many ever years ahead you may want it to be) when you have successfully combined money with service through the offerings of that particular project. You will now do an interview role play with this future imagined version of yourself.

This interview should be done with another person (with the other person playing interviewer and you playing the role of your future self). The interview questions[3] should broadly be related to:

---

[3] If you don't have a friend to do this interview with, you can download a longer list of specific questions and journal your answers to it (writing as if you are your future self). The question list can be found here - https://craftingourlives.com/book-resouces/

1. Circumstances that led up to the particular project/business idea

2. Balancing the creation of a positive impact with financial success

3. Challenges faced and lessons learned while combining wealth creation with service goals

This is literally pretend play! Get playful, fun, and imaginative, and don't hesitate to be bold while making up your answers. There might be times when the interview will not feel like fun. There will be doubts that creep up, resistance that you may feel, or discomfort that stems in your mind.

These resistances are what will point you toward your own limiting beliefs, and it is essential that you pay attention to them. For only then can you start working on these limiting beliefs, and the whole purpose of this exercise is not to actually do this one particular fictional project but rather to get past your limiting beliefs in your mind. Once these beliefs begin to fall away, you will realize that you can easily bring this integrative and abundant mindset into more and more of your future work offerings.

Exercise #3: Pod Discussion

Just as in the previous chapters, share and discuss with your Pod, whatever you might have experienced or discovered through the above exercises.

Talk openly about the outcome of your mind map exercise, what your future self thought about the integration of wealth creation with service, as well as any resistances that came up during the interview.

Specifically discuss the following:

1. How can the presence of wealth facilitate or positively contribute to a joyous and fulfilling work environment and experience? How can it help you move forward in your personalized journey of success?

2. Can there be a connecting thread of joy in money, work, service, and your personal definition of success? How can the alignment of these create a positive feedback loop, reinforcing the joy derived from each aspect?

In the world of career crafting, embracing abundance goes beyond just counting money—it's about celebrating how well you've aligned your talents with creating real value for others. Because people will only pay you, when you touch their lives or create more value for them.

When you start receiving financial rewards for your hard work, see it as a chance to build a stronger foundation for your future. It's like a beautiful cycle: by investing in yourself and using your wealth to upgrade your work, you can contribute better to others and when you do that, they will pay you more for your services.

You can use your abundance to fuel your personal growth, expand your business reach and make a difference in the world. You can also use it to support and empower others, contributing to a larger unfolding of shared success and joy. *Just think of all the positive impact you could create with more abundance!*

6

Manoeuvring your Lizard Brain

"Almost everything will work again if you unplug it for a few minutes, including you."

Anne Lamott

We humans like to think of ourselves as the smartest creatures on Earth, with our brains giving us a unique edge. And for the most part, that's true… but there's more to it. Our brains, as fantastic and wonderful as they are, have two sides. We often assume that the more evolved, rational side is what's steering the ship, but we tend to overlook the other side—the side that wields surprising influence over us.

This other side, often called the lizard brain, is what we're going to explore in this chapter.

So, why the funny name? While it's commonly referred to as the 'lizard brain,' psychologists prefer the term 'reptilian brain.' It's the most primitive part of our brain, sitting right at the base of the brain stem. And you might be wondering: if it's so primitive, why does it matter? Why should we pay attention to it?

Here's why: this reptilian brain can sneak into the driver's seat of our thinking and decision-making, especially when it really counts in our careers and lives. It can even mess with our thoughts during ordinary moments, turning a perfectly smooth situation into one where we trip ourselves up.

Learning to manage our lizard brain is crucial, because like it or not, we can't get rid of it. And honestly, we wouldn't want to. It's there for a reason, rooted in our evolution, and it's going to step in at certain times. So even though we have really smart and advanced parts of our brain that we'd prefer to use when making decisions, they're not always the ones running the show.

Now, the big question is: when does this lizard brain take over?

It steps in when we're under stress. In those nail-biting, high-pressure moments when we most need to be sharp and clear-headed, this primitive part of our brain tends to take control.

But is this really the mindset we want to rely on when we're dealing with stress in our work and careers? Do we want to make snap decisions or lose our cool when a tough assignment lands on our desk or a meeting goes sideways? Absolutely not!

That's why it's so important to understand this lizard brain, learn how to navigate it, and make sure it doesn't hijack your thinking every time stress rears its head. My goal is to help you keep your lizard brain from sabotaging your career crafting journey. I know this is no easy task because there will be plenty of times (and it still happens to me as well) when that reptilian brain will try to take center stage.

For such situations, I want to empower you to be mindful enough to at least not take rash actions, or make critical choices related to your career when your lizard brain is in the driving seat.

Decoding Stress & Its Evolutionary Origins

To really get a handle on the lizard brain, we first need to understand stress—what is it, when does it arise, and why. Stress is a term we all toss around pretty casually, and while we each have our unique stress triggers, and it shows up in different ways for everyone, the core of it is the same. At its heart, stress is the body-mind system's reaction to a perceived threat. And here's the key word: *perceived*. The stress response is designed to kick in even before we can confirm that there's a real danger lurking.

Let's rewind to the days of cavemen, to really understand the logic behind our internal stress wiring. Imagine that Person A and Person B (two hypothetical cavemen with differing biological designs) are strolling through a jungle when they hear some rustling in the bushes. Through the dense greenery, they catch glimpses of brown-orange fur. Person A immediately thinks, "Tiger!" and bolts. Person B, on the other hand, pauses to think and deliberate about what they saw, and in that moment, they miss the chance to escape. In this situation (and others that our ancestors faced daily), who's more likely to survive? Of course, it's Person A.

Something just clicked in Person A's brain—a switch flipped, warning them there was a tiger in those bushes, and they ran. This is the switch that gave control to the lizard brain. This switch was missing in Person B, who continued to operate in their normal mode. Think of our brain as having different modes, much like a smartphone. Person A's brain quickly switched into stress mode / lizard brain and that's what helped them make a fast escape.

When we slip into stress mode (with the lizard brain in control), a whole range of physiological and biological changes kick in. Our brain sends out distress signals that trigger the release of specific hormones, which act as catalysts to influence various processes in our body - so that we can deal with the perceived threat better.

It's a really well designed system that nature has created for our stress response. Our breathing rate increases as does our heart rate - taking in more oxygen and getting our blood pumping faster, and releasing more glucose to give us that sudden burst of energy.

Our stress hormones also temporarily suppresses certain functions that would otherwise use up precious energy. Functions like digestion, growth, reproduction, and even parts of our immune system (whose job is to fight off tiny viruses rather than a big tiger) are deprioritized.

But it's not just physical changes that happen in stress mode— our minds undergo some shifts too, altering our thinking, perception, and focus. In a stressed mode, our thinking shifts to basic, rudimentary analysis, black and white thinking, and quick impulsive judgments—all characteristic of the lizard brain. But do remember, this is the kind of thinking that actually helped Person A escape.

We've also learned about bounded awareness—our mind's ability to focus on a select few stimuli while ignoring the rest. When we're under stress, this awareness becomes even more narrowed. Just like, person A focused solely on the possible tiger.

Now imagine further that Person A, after escaping the first tiger, sees another bush rustling. There could be many possible interpretations of this neutral phenomenon, but the most cautious interpretation for person A's brain would be to assume another tiger is there, or that the same one has followed them - and this would make him run away from the second bush as well. This is an example of 'worst-case thinking', 'pessimism' and 'doubt'— additional mental changes that happen in the stress mode.

So, the stress mode brings impulsive decisions, black and white thinking, a narrowed viewpoint, and pessimism. Not a very desirable mode is it?

There are some fringe benefits in the stress mode though, especially because of the narrowed awareness. Stress can help us focus on the task at hand, pushing aside distractions. However, it's crucial to remember that this focus comes at a price—a severe one paid by your body due to the suppression of vital functions necessary for your well being. Functions like digestion, growth, immunity, repair and reproduction. Also look at some of the modern day diseases like hypertension or diabetes and you can see how they are related to the changes that occur in the stress mode like increased blood pressure or glucose.

Every time I discuss this topic in my workshops, someone always claims that stress boosts their productivity. And my response is, "You're right, but it's a short-term boost that comes with long-term damage to your health." Plus, you could suffer bigger setbacks and make costly mistakes, if you make critical decisions with your simplistic lizard brain, instead of your smarter and more evolved brain.

What many people don't realize is that the focus and drive that stress provides can also be achieved in other ways. Remember the concept of 'flow' we discussed in Chapter 4? When we're in a state of flow, our brain is highly focused and motivated, just like in stress mode, but without the fear. The stress hormones aren't activated, so your body functions aren't compromised. In a state of flow, you get the same benefits of productivity and focus—minus the costs that stress brings.

Managing Stressors at Work

Much as we would like to eliminate stress and stressors from our work and lives, these are never going to completely go away. The key is then to learn to manage stressors effectively, and to manage our own response to stress, when it does arise.

Our stressors at work are not the same as a tiger lurking in the bushes. They are, in fact, often more benign looking, everyday events—an item suddenly added to your to-do list, having to rework something, or the nervous anticipation of a sit-down with your boss. It can be anything that you perceive as a threat that pushes you into the panic mode and triggers the stress response.

If we revisit one important, distinguishing feature of stress, it becomes clear that our *perception* plays a big role in us feeling stressed. So by altering our mindset and focusing on the positive aspects, we can reduce feelings of being threatened or overwhelmed. Ultimately though, the best way to really deal with potential stressors is to become fearless enough to not see those specific situations or events as threats anymore.

However, reaching this place of ultimate fearlessness and zen-like indifference to potential stressors can require years and years of inner work. We are all somewhere along that journey. So on that journey, we can rest assured that there will be enough times, where our brains will interpret something as a perceived threat and the stress response will be activated and our lizard brain will come into the driving seat. What do we do then? Fortunately we have some simple switching techniques to use at those moments, (helping us regain control from our lizard brain) and we shall learn about these at the end of this chapter. Before that however, I want to educate you about a unique kind type of workplace stress to look out for.

Multitasking and ADT

Attention Deficit Trait (ADT), a term coined by Psychiatrist Edward Hallowell, is a unique type of workplace stress where there's no single, specific trigger. Instead, it's caused by multiple, simultaneous demands on our attention. The key difference between ADT and traditional stress lies in their origins. Traditional stress is triggered by an external threat (real or perceived). In contrast, ADT is an internal reaction—our brain's panic response to multitasking and constant demands. Although our reaction to both types of stress is similar (our 'lizard brain' takes over), the triggers come from different places.

Let me share one of my own 'wake-up moments' with ADT. I was working from home on a dream project, but I wasn't just working. Part of my mind was listening for the cooker whistles in the kitchen, another was distracted by a Facebook message from a friend announcing her engagement, and yet another part got pulled away by a text chime about money credited to my account. I was surrounded by good news and in a happy place, but my brain was juggling too many things at once, and that was my undoing.

Just then, my young son came running up to show me a drawing he'd made. My already overloaded brain gave in, and I snapped at him. I felt stressed, not because of any real crisis, but simply because my brain was trying to do too many tasks simultaneously. And snapping at my son, who did nothing wrong, pushed me straight into a guilt spiral.

That's the paradox of ADT—it can sneak up on you even in moments of joy. What we don't realize is that our frontal lobes (the most evolved part of the brain that we use for executive functioning) are excellent at serial processing, but not at parallel processing. When we think we are multitasking, our brain is actually just time-slicing, and all that extra switching effort contributes to its overload.

The good news is, recovering from ADT is much quicker and easier than from conventional stress. With regular stress, the triggers keep coming until you do some deep inner work to tackle the fear or threat. But with ADT, once you recognize it, all you need to do is stop multitasking to prevent your brain from getting overwhelmed again. Simple tweaks like closing extra tabs on your laptop, putting your phone away, or better scheduling your time can make a world of difference to your well-being and performance.

Is Your Stress Really Yours?

We all know what the feeling of being stressed is like. Based on certain telltale signs that we each identify for ourselves, we know when we're stressed.

But what we don't always know is whether it is truly us that is stressed, or whether we are simply feeling the emotion of stress due to signals that we are picking up from others. And the latter happens more number of times than we can imagine.

A lab study on monkeys led to the accidental discovery of a very unique type of neurons in our brains. The researchers were mapping brain activity to understand which areas activated during specific actions. During the experiment, one researcher observed something unusual: a monkey's brain showed activation in the region typically associated with arm movements, even though the monkey was perfectly still. Upon closer inspection, they realized that the monkey was intently watching a person outside the window who was making repetitive arm movements. The monkey's brain cells related to arm movements were firing in response to simply observing this action.

This startling observation led to a series of experiments on the human brain, which unveiled a new class of neurons, aptly named "mirror neurons." These neurons are activated not only when we perform an action but also when we witness someone else doing it. When we watch someone smile, our mirror neurons activate as if we were smiling ourselves. When we witness another person in stress or panic, our own brain mimics that as well. In essence, mirror neurons embody our brain's remarkable ability to reflect and resonate with the experiences of others.

It was always known that we are social beings. However, with mirror neurons, we started understanding just how contagiously social we are. While interacting with other humans, we pass on moods, thoughts, and even our neural configurations. The evolutionary purpose and dedicated job of mirror neurons seems to be to make us aware of the emotions of other people.

But here's what often happens because of these mirror neurons: our brain can shift into stress mode, causing us to feel panic and anxiety even when there's no direct threat. This occurs because our brain mirrors the stress experienced by those around us. When their lizard brains are active, our own lizard brains can become activated through mirroring. This activation triggers a downward spiral of judgmental and fearful thinking (remember the shifts in our lens and sensemaking when the lizard brain takes control?), eventually making us feel genuinely afraid or threatened. As a result, we end up creating real and seemingly legitimate stress for ourselves.

The idea that others' stress can also, literally, put you in a state of stress is quite alarming. But luckily for you (and all of us who can be affected by this contagion due to mirror neurons) there's an easy fix to it. We need to remain aware and mindful of our internal states and at the first signs of stress ask, *"is this mine or am I mirroring someone else?"* Bringing your awareness to what your true feelings were just before you experienced that sudden onslaught of stress is often a great way to check if something has truly triggered you or whether your brain is simply reflecting the stressed feelings of someone else.

Regaining Control

Now that we've explored the causes and consequences of stress and how our lizard brain can take over, let's focus on how to take back the reins. This is a crucial aspect of our inner sovereignty, isn't it? It's about mastering the art of quickly switching gears and preventing our lizard brain from pushing us into impulsive decisions or choices we might later regret.

To regain control, we need to switch out of the stress mode. Think of it like turning your phone from ringer mode to silent — it instantly changes the way it functions. In the same way, shifting out of stress mode helps you avoid the typical behaviours that come with it, like rash decisions and tunnel vision.

Once you make this switch, your frontal lobes are back in charge, giving you the power to think clearly, make smarter decisions, and truly act from a place of strength.

Exercise #1

This first exercise entails trying out various switching techniques and finding a few that work well for you. Prepare a handy toolkit for yourself that contains 3-4 such methods (you can have more, but you don't need more than these).

There are quite a few ways that this switch can be made. My favorite is to make my breath an anchor and leverage the power of deep breathing. This is a physiological switch and almost always works. You see our body-mind-system associates fast breathing with the stress mode, and slow breathing with a normal mode. Hence by switching our breath pattern, we trick the rest of this interconnected system to also switch back into our normal mode.

Cognitive restructuring (replacing stress-producing thoughts with more balanced thoughts), imagining a calming scenario (guided visualization), laughing out loud, splashing cold water on your face, or connecting with nature are other simple but effective ways to help you make this switch.

If none of the above appeal to you, refer to the book resources section for a longer list[4] of Switching Techniques that you can experiment with.

Learning to recognize when your lizard brain is getting active, and practising the art of trying to switch out from it will positively impact your life in more ways than one. I am not saying that even after learning about it you will always be able to switch out of it.

---

[4] You can access a list of 20 switching techniques, with explanation for why they work in the book resources page: https://craftingourlives.com/book-resouces/

However, with practice you will be able to start doing it more often and also doing it quicker.

And once you're able to do so, you are likely to see your efficiency skyrocket. You will have much more *'genius time'* on your hands; the relaxed time when you're functioning from the most intelligent, creative, resourceful, and highest-thinking part of your brain.

I cannot stress the importance of manoeuvring your lizard brain and using these switching techniques enough. How much ever progress you may make in your career alchemy journey, it will all be ineffective if you cannot control your reptilian brain. A lot of the methods and practices that we have discussed thus far, and which we will discuss going ahead, can be used only by the more evolved and smarter parts of your brain. However, if that brain is always in the back seat while the lizard brain is steering you, how will you be able to truly benefit from your career crafting experience?

I have learned this over the years in the hard way, but I believe I am getting better. I too have my moments of operating from my lizard brain, but I am better equipped now to recognize it and switch out from it. I hope for the same for you—so that you can regain control and live, work, and make your choices more and more from the most empowered and effective states of your being.

Exercise #2: Pod Discussion

Now it's time to bring your experience to your Pod and hear about theirs. Share what you've learned from trying out different switching techniques. Talk about what worked well for you, what didn't, and how you went about experimenting with these methods.

By sharing and listening, you'll broaden your understanding and also get new ideas and confidence (through hearing others' success stories) on how these techniques can be adapted to different situations.

Exercise #3: Habits for Ongoing Stress Management

So far, we've explored what to do once the lizard brain seizes control. But let's rewind a bit: is there a way to keep it from hijacking our thinking in the first place?

We know we can't eliminate the lizard brain. It's a part of us—designed to keep us safe from threats. It's going to rear its head from time to time. But what we can do is build habits and routines that make it less likely to take over. Since this primitive part of our brain is fuelled by stress, we want to focus on practices that lower our overall stress levels.

Of course, these routines will not completely erase stress—but they can improve our stress baseline. There's a reason that so many people swear by having practices like meditation, exercise, or a proper diet in their daily lives, for they bring unparalleled benefits.

My own 'must includes' for a stress-resilient routine include meditation, breathwork, exercise, healthy eating, enough sleep, socializing and time in nature. I encourage you to create your own (You can access a list of suggested practices in the additional resources page)[5].

My ultimate goal here is to put you in a better position to tackle stress and stressors. They have always been there and will always remain there. In fact, we know that in some cases, there doesn't

---

[5] https://craftingourlives.com/book-resouces/

even need to be anything out there that makes us stressed, for we create triggers internally (through multitasking or otherwise), or we might even just be mirroring the stress of others. But as and when stress comes, my hope is that you can navigate such times with the most powerful parts of your brain and make the wisest and most informed decisions for yourself.

7

Navigating Failure & Cultivating Resilience

"It is impossible to live without failing at something, unless you live so cautiously that you might as well not have lived at all - in which case, you fail by default."

- J. K. Rowling

Failure is a term that evokes a deep-seated fear in many of us, a fear that often looms large and can stop us in our tracks. From our earliest days, we've been conditioned to see failure as something to be avoided at all costs. Remember the anxiety of cramming for exams, driven by the fear of a poor grade? This fear of failure, ingrained from childhood, follows us into adulthood, casting a long shadow over our professional and personal lives.

But is failure really the devil that we have made it out to be? Or can it be revisited with a different lens, one that will give us a clearer picture and let us see it for the other roles that it can play in our lives?

And what is the interplay of failure and resilience?

These are some of the questions that we shall explore in this chapter.

Adopting an Infinite Perspective

Think about sports like basketball or cricket. These are classic examples of finite games—there's a clear goal, a score to settle, and a winner to declare. Or take competitive exams like NEET or JEE. The target is defined, and achieving it means you've won that particular challenge. It's straightforward, measurable, and if you fall short, it's easy to say you didn't meet the mark.

But life and your career? They don't quite follow that playbook. They're more like an ongoing, infinite game. Sure, you might lose a job, miss out on a promotion, or stumble in a project. But here's the thing: there will always be more jobs, more promotions, and more projects on the horizon. And, ideally, you'll use the lessons, experiences, and resilience you gained from that previous stumble to nail the next opportunity that comes your way. This is what makes your career an infinite journey. And in this infinite journey, failure takes on a whole new meaning.

Remember our discussion on the Hero's Journey? It's pretty rare to find someone whose career has been nothing but smooth sailing, a path marked by win after win. But if you do happen to be one of those rare folks, let me toss this thought your way: is it possible that your career is win-heavy because you haven't yet pushed your limits or taken those big innovative risks? When you step outside your comfort zone or try something new, the very natural odds dictate that some things will be a hit and some will be a miss. The point that I'm trying to make here is that failure is a completely normal and acceptable part of your infinite career game.

I want to help you see this real face of failure, and in the process, strip away the fear associated with it and reduce the pain and sting that often comes with it. I want to broaden your perspective so that you start seeing failure not as a problem, but as an opportunity—a chance for feedback, learning, growth, gaining wisdom, and most importantly, building resilience.

By embracing an infinite game perspective, failure can start to look less like a roadblock and more like a stepping stone on your life and career journey. Only when we stop seeing it as a problem, and more for the opportunity it actually carries to transform our life and career, will we actually be open to receive the gifts that failure has to offer.

When we see our life and career as an infinite adventure, new opportunities are always on the horizon, giving us endless chances to bounce back, learn, and grow from past missteps.

Overcoming the Fear of Failure

Let me ask you a question here: Between a person who has only tasted wins and someone who has experienced both wins and losses, who will be more likely to have a more intense fear of failure? Perhaps you think it will be the second person. After all, since the first one has already been successful so many times, why should he/she be scared to fail once?

But here's the big reveal—my years of experience have shown me the opposite. Through countless interactions with students, course participants, and coaching clients (many of whom hail from top-notch institutions or work in prestigious companies), I've noticed a surprising trend. The more qualified a person is and the more past wins they've had, the more they seem to be crippled by the fear of failure. This is the kind of delusional hold it has over us; it can make us forget our many accomplishments and trap us in a loop of anxiety about one unfavourable thing that might come our way.

To give the devil its due, the fear of failure can sometimes act as a motivator—forcing us into action, making sure we burn the midnight oil, and get things done. But, it is not the only way, and definitely not the best way to motivate either ourselves or others.

Let's circle back to our discussion on stress and the reptilian brain. Remember how our stress response is triggered by a perceived threat? And a threat naturally pushes us into a corner of fear. Connect the dots, and it's clear that, like stress, our lizard brain takes the wheel when we're acting under any kind of fear (including the fear of failure). And as we've explored, this is not great news for our decision-making or thinking.

Imagine you're working on a project. Instead of approaching it with a positive or neutral mindset, you let the fear of failure take over. When that happens, the smarter, more evolved part of your brain steps aside, and your thoughts, actions, and decisions are no longer your best. Because of this, the fear of failure actively undermines your performance, which in turn increases your chances of actually failing.

Also, under the effect of this fear, it's as if our brains are operating on a subconscious algorithm of *'avoid failure at any cost.'* So we tend to favor tasks that offer easy, guaranteed success and shy away from exploring new ideas or projects—blocking ourselves from seizing opportunities in areas where we risk the unknown.

So, we know this fear isn't really helping us, but how can we overcome it? The good news is that the fear of failure is completely man-made. It didn't exist in nature, and it's not something we're born with—it's something we've developed over time. It's a product of our conditioning, a result of the frameworks through which our brains have been taught to view failure. And frames can be reframed, and conditioning can be unconditioned! Even if you cannot let it go completely, you can loosen the grip that this fear has on you.

Here are four approaches I recommend for this process of unconditioning. You don't have to use all of them. Instead, pick one or two that resonate with you, and keep practicing until they become second nature for your brain.

1. Adopt a Prototyping Mindset

This approach stems from the world of business; in particular, from design thinking. Think of every stage of your career as a prototype testing of yourself- something that is not the final version, but that is going to keep getting better and stronger. With this mindset, there won't be any definite success or failure for you, because you will always be on a constant journey toward betterment and growth.

2. Take your Older Self's Perspective

Coming from the field of psychology, this approach recommends looking at situations from a different perspective, as your older self would.

A study conducted on people in their 70s revealed that the things they regretted most in their old age were not the things they failed in, but rather the things that they never tried doing because of the fear of failure. And hence, this approach asks you to put yourself in the shoes of an older you. Would you rather have the regret of never trying out things, or the satisfaction that you tried everything you wanted, some of which led to success and some to failure? Realizing that the second option is the better one will help you make braver choices when you are faced with the fear of failure.

3.　Invest in the Journey

This is a simple but powerful refocussing technique. As the name suggests, it entails acknowledging the journey that you have already endured on your way toward your goal. It entails appreciating the process and the wonderful things that you are gaining or learning with every step.

When you focus only on the goal and nothing else, it will be much more devastating for you to cope with failure (and the subsequent fear of it) in case it comes your way. But when you also invest in the journey, the failure (and fear of it) seem much easier to handle since you know that even if you do not win, you do not lose everything either.

4.　Non-Judgment

This is one of my personal favourite approaches that has its origins in Buddhist philosophy. While Non-Judgement, by itself is a mindset that has many benefits for our inner and outer worlds, there is a specific zen parable that I like to narrate which best encapsulates its role in terms of helping us change our outlook on failure.

In fact many of my students forget the stance, but remember the story—and that remembrance itself helps them. I distinctly remember a student running across the college lawns during her stressful final placements to ask me to re-tell this story to her that very moment. Here's the parable:

There lived a farmer in a village, and one day his favorite horse ran away. His neighbours gathered around and lamented, "Your horse ran away. How unfortunate!" The farmer only said, *"Good thing, bad thing, who knows"*. A few days later, the horse returned home, with three strong wild horses in tow. "What good fortune. What incredible luck," the villagers exclaimed. *"Good thing, bad thing, who knows,"* the farmer again replied. The following week, the farmer's son was trying to tame one of the wild horses, when he fell off and fractured his leg. The villagers arrived to express their dismay. "What dismal luck," they said. *"Good thing, bad thing, who knows,"* the farmer replied again. The next month, a military officer marched into the village, recruiting able-bodied young men for the war. The farmer's son, with his broken leg, was left behind. The villagers were joyful, "Your son has been spared. What beautiful luck!" The farmer simply smiled. *"Good thing, bad thing, who knows."*

The lesson I've taken from this story is that, despite our instinct to label things as 'good' or 'bad,' our brains can never grasp the full picture or foresee what the future holds. We can find a lot of relief by consciously choosing to stay in a place of non-judgment, especially when the world around us is quick to call something a 'bad thing' simply because it didn't go as planned.

Life often surprises us, and what seems like a failure today might be laying the groundwork for a bigger success tomorrow. So why confine our understanding by slapping rigid labels on events? When you decide in advance that something is 'bad,' you're more likely to sink into despair, avoid reflecting on it, and miss the chance to learn from it. But with a neutral mindset, you can acknowledge that things didn't go as expected and find constructive ways to move forward. This openness allows you to see every experience as a source of wisdom and growth, and over time, it becomes second nature to approach challenges with this healthier perspective.

The Road Towards Resilience

Setbacks, failures, and crises are a part of this infinite game we are playing. When life knocks us off our feet, coping is the act of getting back up and returning to where we started. But resilience? That's something different altogether. It's not just about bouncing back; it's about bouncing forward. Resilience is what helps us emerge from challenges not just intact, but stronger, smarter, and more capable than before.

Now, I get it. This might sound a little too good to be true. You might be wondering, "Is it really that simple?" The truth is, it's not always a straight line upward. Sometimes, a setback knocks us down, and we stay down. It can send us spiralling into self-doubt, frustration, or even depression. I've been there myself — stuck in that downward spiral, feeling like a victim of circumstance. And that's exactly why I'm passionate about helping people build resilience.

While we are all born with a certain amount of resilience and it is an inherent human quality—there are definite things we can do to cultivate it further.

Inner Resilience

Inner resilience, the strength that stems from our mind, is the most powerful tool we have in our Hero's toolkit. And like any other good quality or capacity, it can be developed through practice. I am going to share three of my favourite inner resilience tools with you below.[6]

1. Explanatory Styles in Mental Chatter

We've all faced failures that felt like the end of the world — whether it was a project that didn't go as planned or a role we didn't quite fit into. And trust me, I've been there too. But it wasn't until I stumbled upon Martin Seligman's work on explanatory styles that I realized how much our own internal thinking can shape our resilience.

Seligman talks about the "Three Ps"—permanence, pervasiveness, and personalization—that influence how we interpret failures.

Let's say you've stumbled on a project at work. If you're telling yourself, "This didn't work out, but I can do better next time," you're treating the failure as a temporary blip, not a defining moment. But if your inner narrative says, "I failed, and now my career is over," you're seeing this setback as a permanent state. The trick is to resist labelling any setback as a final verdict on your future. The less permanent you make it, the more resilient you become.

Now, consider how failure can spread. You face a challenge at work, and suddenly, it's affecting your mood at home or your

---

[6] You can access an entire masterclass on inner resilience in the book resources page: https://craftingourlives.com/book-resouces/

confidence in other areas. This is the idea of pervasiveness — when a problem in one part of life starts to overshadow everything else. To stay resilient, you need to contain that setback to where it belongs. Don't let a bad day at work color your entire week or spill into your relationships. Keeping boundaries around the impact of failure helps you recover faster and keeps your sense of self intact.

Lastly, think about how you interpret failures. Do you tend to blame yourself for every mistake, taking full responsibility even when it's not entirely in your control? That's personalization — the habit of assuming that every failure is a reflection of your worth. But if you step back and recognize that setbacks often involve multiple factors, you'll find it easier to move forward. It's not about denying your role in what happened, but about understanding that failure is rarely just about you. It's about seeing the bigger picture and realizing you're not alone in the story.

The key is to pay attention to how you're framing setbacks in your mind. Are you turning them into lifelong scars, allowing them to overshadow everything else, or shouldering all the blame? As you begin to start catching yourself in these patterns and reframe your inner narratives, you'll find yourself building true inner resilience.

2.   Focus Within Circle of Control

Broadly speaking, the situations we find ourselves in or the experiences that happen to us can be categorized as either being within our circle of concern, influence, or control.

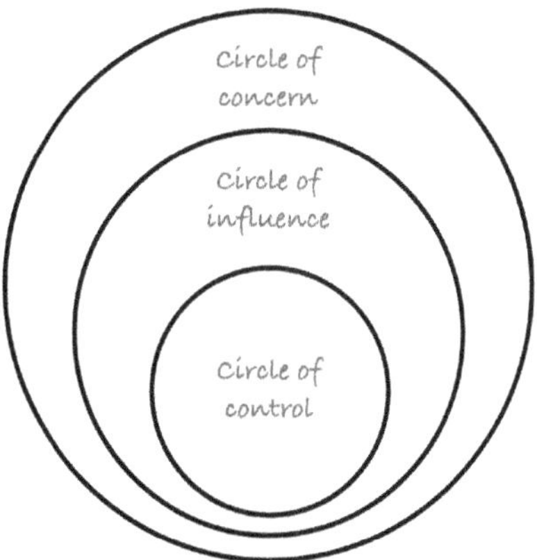

Think of circumstances like natural calamities, or the Covid pandemic. We are all extremely concerned about such events, for they deeply impact our lives, but there is no influence or control we can have over them. Next are the things that we can exert influence upon but which we cannot directly control, such as our work or relationships. The outcome is not in our hands, but we can take measures toward securing the outcome that we want. Last come the things that are directly in our control, such as our daily habits, what kind of lifestyle we create for ourselves, how we think, etc.

In times when there is no stress or crisis, I would urge you to divide your time and energy mostly between the things that are within your circles of influence and control. This is because thinking a lot about the things in your ring of concern (but outside your zone of control or influence) is likely to make you dejected, unhappy, or anxious because despite obsessing so much over them, there is nothing you can do about them. I am not asking you to never be there, but merely to limit your time there.

However, when you are dealing with a crisis or setback, I would ask you to focus even more on the things which are actually within your circle of control. It will give you a sense of progress, the satisfaction of having achieved something, and also seeing some results.

This framework further helps me detach from anxiety about the final outcome, because outcomes are usually outside my circle of control. However, the effort that I choose to put in, is always within my circle of control and so focussing on that gives me strength to keep moving on, especially in difficult times.

3. Meaning & Purpose

A strong sense of purpose or a personal mission can also increase our resilience, especially during life's rough patches. Victor Frankl's groundbreaking research, carried out under the extreme conditions of a World War II concentration camp, uncovered a critical insight: people who could anchor their experiences to a deeper sense of purpose were better equipped to handle extreme adversity and find hope even in the midst of despair.

Modern neuroscience adds another layer of insight. It shows that having a clear personal mission or purpose activates the brain regions associated with reward and motivation—yes, even when we're facing challenges. This means that when we encounter failure or setbacks, our sense of purpose serves as a psychological buffer, helping us stay focused and motivated.

Whenever I face a failure or setback, I make it a habit to connect with my mission (which, for me, is to de-villainize work on this planet) and remind myself of its relevance despite the current disappointment. This practice is incredibly effective at transforming my emotional energy from frustration (or even despair) into motivation. It helps me shift my focus from dwelling on the pain of past failures to thinking about what's needed next. This way, I can move forward with renewed determination and clarity, ready to tackle the next steps on my journey.

And so, I hope for each of you to experience the immense power and resilience that comes from creating a mission or purpose for yourself. You can build these through combining insights from the values exercises that you did in chapter 3.

Do remember however that in order to work, your mission or purpose has to be internally resonant for you. Sometimes, other people around us (gurus, teachers, parents, preachers) might tell us what mission or purpose we are supposed to have in life. If their suggestion is one that resonates with your heart and truly convinces you, you will surely be able to derive resilience from it. However, if that is not the case and you simply parrot that as your purpose out of respect or trust in the other person, the benefit of resilience that I have talked about will not find its way to you.

Resilience from the Outside

There is, undoubtedly, a reservoir of resilience within us that we can draw strength from when we are down. But, help can also be found on the outside. Our family, friends, colleagues, and social networks can provide support, fresh perspectives, and encouragement when we're feeling down. This type of support, which I like to call outer resilience, isn't just about luck, its something we can deliberately cultivate and nurture—our personalized resilience network.

Any network thrives on the mutual exchange of support and value. It's not just about leaning on others when times are tough but also about being there for them in their moments of need. I do want to remind you however, that interacting with others can either pull us down or lift us up. It can go either ways, and therefore to help you nurture a 'lift you up' network, (as opposed to a 'drag you down network'), I want to suggest four areas to focus on (Relationships, Efficacy, Affect, and Learning), easily remembered through the acronym - REAL.

1. Relationships

The first step to building a resilience network is to create meaningful bonds with others. Add value and nurture the relationships that you have, be it through a regular phone call to check in on people, or making space in your schedule to spend time with them.

Once you have the bond in place start turning these into parts of your 'lift you up network' by further including the following three aspects - Efficacy, Affect and Learning.

2. Efficacy

Efficacy is largely like self-esteem, but it is a bit more specific than that. It is about having goals and aspirations, as well as the confidence that they can be achieved. It is very closely linked to the concept of meaning and purpose which is crucial for the development of inner resilience.

It is important that you, along with the other people you work and live with, have efficacy. It energizes us whenever we hit a roadblock and contributes to the development of resilience.

So, how can efficacy be developed? You can start with simple but significant measures like creating goals or specific targets or keeping track of your progress toward these. And most importantly, talk to other people about it. Share your journey milestones and ask about theirs. It is about instilling a sense of belief in yourself that your time and efforts matter, and doing the same for others too.

3. Affect

The power of positivity is something that we have all heard about and even experienced at some point in our lives. When we, and even those around us are positive (remember how mirror neurons reflect the emotions of those around us?), we can think more creatively, find better solutions, and cope in a healthier way with stress.

Affect means creating positivity in yourself and those around you so everyone can reap the numerous benefits that come with it. An important distinction here is between making yourself responsible for someone else's happiness (which is not what I am asking you to do) versus simply trying to spread happiness. The first option is something that can only reside in your circle of influence but not your control because another person's ultimate emotional state might not always end up in the way you intend. But your efforts are solely in your hands, so just focus on that.

Use gratitude and appreciation[7] to show the people around you that their efforts matter to you, and acknowledge all the good things they have done. It is equally important to acknowledge yourself too for the things you do well. Whoever (either you or others) is the recipient of this gratitude, you will undoubtedly feel a surge of positive emotions and also a sense of efficacy through this practice.

---

[7] Watch my TED talk on this topic in the additional resources page:
https://craftingourlives.com/book-resouces/

4. Learning

This is, once again, a personal favourite, and for a very good reason too. I believe it can be followed anywhere and everywhere; nothing can take away your ability, power, desire, and intent to learn. Learning is always in your control and you can do it in times of wins or losses, in times of happiness or stress, and by yourself or with others—the possibilities are limitless.

And the most wonderful part of learning is that it has a ripple effect and enhances all the other three aspects too. Learning about something or someone gives you a sense of positive affect, it boosts your efficacy by giving a sense of accomplishment, and learning with or about others is a great way to add value and strengthen relationships.

Keeping the spirit of learning alive in your interactions with people in your resilience network is a great win-win strategy that can never let you down.

Exercise #1: Discovery Interviews on Failure

Find a partner and take turns interviewing each other about a time you felt you failed. Ask them to describe a specific incident, and then switch roles and let them interview you as you share your own story of failure and the lessons it taught you.

You have the complete freedom to choose your interviewer (and subsequent interviewee) for this exercise. It can, of course, be one of your Pod members but this is not mandatory. The exercise can also be done with a parent, spouse, friend, or colleague who has not read this book as long as you share just this section with them.

As the interviewee, your task is simple: Go with the flow and just share your story. However, when you are the interviewer, there are certain essentials to keep in mind. These naturally apply to the person conducting your interview too.

First and foremost, it is important to maintain a safe space. The culture of human society and our past conditioning have made failure a topic of taboo; we do not usually discuss it. In fact, we avoid even openly acknowledging it to ourselves. So, it is essential to create a safe and sacred place where the other person can be comfortable and vulnerable enough to discuss their failures.

The second is to be actively listening to them and embodying empathy. Ask questions to clarify and broaden your understanding of their experience, and in this sense, it is alright to interrupt their narration. However, I implore you not to interrupt them just for the sake of it, for this will disrupt their flow.

Lastly, you need to be strict with yourself so as to not offer advice, counselling, suggestions, or solutions of any kind to your interviewee. When someone is sharing their struggles with us, we often slip into the zone of wanting to help them by recommending measures they can take, books they can read, or mindsets that they can adopt. While this comes from a good place, it will undermine the effectiveness of this exercise.

To guide you through this unique interview, here is a list of key questions that you should cover during the discussion. Make sure to explore each question thoroughly, as doing so is crucial for gaining the full insights that this activity offers.

1. Recount one event from your life where you failed at something but eventually learned something from that experience—describe the event.

2. What were some of the setbacks you experienced as a result of this event?

3. What were your thoughts, feelings, and behaviors immediately after this experience?

4. What mechanisms helped you cope with the setback? These could be in self, in others, or in the systems around you.

5. To what extent did these mechanisms help in restoring your well-being?

6. What did you learn about yourself/others/ about the situation or industry from this experience?

7. Try to think of ways in which this event and coping with it helped you grow and made you stronger.

Your task for this exercise does not end with taking and giving an interview. After you are done with both rounds of the interview, it is essential to find some quiet time with your thoughts and journal your experience. I strongly recommend trying to complete this journaling immediately after the interview, so that your thoughts remain raw, unfiltered, and free of analysis or judgment. Pen down how you felt while narrating your story and hearing the other person's story, as well as about what your concept of 'failure' looks like after the interviews.

You can repeat this interview with multiple people (recalling different failure incidents from your own life each time you do the exercise). At the end (of how many ever interviews you do), write a letter to a younger version of yourself explaining how you would like that young child (pick an age between 8 and 16) to look at failure. Turn back the wheels of time and through this letter, offer your hypothetical younger self all the wisdom about failure that you have gained now.

<u>Exercise #2: Nurturing Your Resilience Network</u>

Step 1: Think about the different people in your current support system and reflect on the various kinds of support that you approach them for—whether it's for boosting your confidence, finding a way forward, providing a sympathetic ear for your negative emotions, or reminding you of your purpose and mission in your career or life. Perhaps there is someone who helps you find humour in a tough situation and makes you laugh, or someone who broadens your perspective and helps you reframe things.

Step 2: Identify specific categories of support where you'd like to strengthen your relationships from a resilience perspective. This could involve creating and nurturing new connections that meet these needs or adding a new dimension of communication and interaction to existing relationships.

Step 3: Make a deliberate plan to consciously grow the 'give' aspect of the 'give and take' in your resilience network. This means finding ways to support others and being a source of resilience in their lives, continuing the symbiotic relationship of mutual upliftment.

Failure isn't the enemy—it's more like an uninvited guest at your career party. It shows up when you least expect it, often overstaying its welcome, but it doesn't have to ruin the celebration. What if, instead of seeing failure as a monster, we saw it as a surprising companion, offering lessons we didn't know we needed? Every setback has the potential to make us a bit more daring, a bit more compassionate with ourselves, and a lot more adaptable. It's in those unexpected moments—when things fall apart—that we find the raw materials for something better, something more true to who we are becoming.

Resilience is like a muscle we build over time. We don't build it by ignoring the pain or pretending we're not struggling; we build it by facing the struggle head-on, taking stock, and using each experience to grow stronger.

8

Co-Working with Inner Voices

""Make sure your own worst enemy doesn't live between your own two ears."

Laird Hamilton

Remember that first exercise we did in this book where we tuned into our mental chatter? Well, let's revisit that because our inner voices can turn into quite the lively cast, especially when we're stepping into new or challenging territory. Sometimes, there's a stern voice chiming in with doubts like, 'Are you sure you can handle this?' Other times, we hear a more anxious whisper asking, 'Is it safe here? Are you sure we're okay?' And don't forget those nagging thoughts that tell us, 'You don't belong here. You're not enough. You'll be found out any minute now.'

But it's not all doom and gloom! We also have some positive voices that can cheer us on. Imagine a voice saying, 'You've got this. Look how far you've come!' or 'Remember that time you overcame a similar challenge? You can do it again!' These voices remind us of our strengths and past successes, giving us a much-needed boost.

Think of these voices as different characters in your head, each with their own style and message. Some may try to protect you by pointing out risks, while others are there to remind you of your strengths and past victories.

In this chapter, we'll explore these different voices, focusing on how they influence our thoughts and actions. By recognizing and understanding them, you'll be better equipped to navigate their messages and use them to your advantage.

Inner Voices and Their Roles

First up, let's talk about the Inner Mentor. This is the voice that cheers you on, and one that's often missing for many of us. So, in addition to exploring why this voice is so valuable, I'll help you create your very own Inner Mentor. Think of it as your personal cheerleader, always ready to lift you up and remind you of your strengths.

Next, we have the voice of the Inner Child. This voice is part of all of us, and it's rooted in our early days of life. Even as we grow up, the thoughts, feelings, and desires from our childhood stick around. Our inner world develops in layers—adding new experiences and wisdom with age—yet the original childlike mental models remain unless we do some deep inner work to reprogram them.

The Inner Child can be a mixed bag. On one hand, it can foster creativity, playfulness, and joy. On the other hand, it might push you towards impulsive decisions based on childhood understanding or fears. Your Inner Child's influence will be unique to you, shaped by your early beliefs and experiences.

Then, there's the Inner Critic. This voice is like an echo from the past—phrases and criticisms we've internalized from others, such as "You can't do this!" or "Why did you mess up?" Sometimes, these remarks come from a place of concern, but our minds often replay them in a harsh, self-judgmental loop. This inner voice can become a demeaning critic, making us doubt ourselves and feel inadequate.

Within the Inner Critic, there are sub-voices, like the Inner Jailor. This one keeps us confined within self-imposed boundaries, stopping us from taking risks or trying new things. Another sub-voice is what we often call Imposter Syndrome. It makes us question our achievements, suggesting that any success is just luck or that we're faking it. For instance, if you receive a promotion, this voice might tell you that you don't truly deserve it, making you feel like a fraud.

The Inner Critic, including the Inner Jailor and Imposter Syndrome, generally limits us. While occasionally they might have a protective intent, more often than not, they're just getting in the way—preventing us from embracing new opportunities and being bold.

But don't worry! You're not stuck with these voices pulling you in different directions. My goal is to help you understand these mental characters and manage them effectively. The key is to recognize when these voices show up, identify their impact, and selectively nurture the helpful aspects of them. So Let's begin the inner work needed to to ensure that our inner voices work for us, and not against us.

The Inner Mentor

As I mentioned earlier, this voice may not even be there for many of us. In which case, it is something that we will consciously and deliberately construct. My goal is to help you build it in a way that becomes consistently functional and supportive for you. The primary motivation behind creating this voice is to have an internal ally and motivator; something that can guide us and support us in challenging or tricky situations.

Exercise #1

This exercise is to be done in two parts. The first part is a visualization exercise, wherein I want you to visualize your future self. You can choose how many ever years you want to jump into the future for this (a five year timespan is what I have found working best for most people but you can choose a longer timespan as well). This is a very sweet and simple exercise and there's no wrong way to do it! Just put yourself in a peaceful place (both physically and mentally), keep a pen and paper handy, and jot down whatever comes to your mind.

You can do this exercise through journaling, drawing, or imagining first with eyes closed and later writing it down. Pick whatever you feel most drawn to. If you prefer to do this through an eyes closed guided visualization, then there is also an audio file that you can download from the book resources page[8]. Be sure to follow up the eyes closed guided visualization with immediate journalling however to note down whatever you see.

This image of where you see yourself and how you see yourself in the future is a blueprint that you can use to create an internal persona or sketch of your inner mentor.

I have, to date, not encountered a single participant for this exercise who has not liked the vision they created when they used

---

[8] https://craftingourlives.com/book-resouces/

the guided audio track. If, however, this does not happen on your first try and you end up seeing a vision that does not quite resonate with you, please attempt this again at a time when you're feeling peaceful and relaxed (and your lizard brain is not active).

Sometimes, the vision becomes so grand and wonderful that participants initially feel wowed by it. But very quickly (and perhaps due to the work of certain other voices we have talked about) the narrative quickly changes to, *"That's too good of a vision…it can't be me!"*

And for this reason, I would urge you to not make your vision smaller or more limited, just because you think that what you first imagined is too big or out of your league. It never is! Just let your thoughts flow freely and as long as you like what you're seeing (or creating, if you are drawing this with open eyes) do not try to limit your sketch in any way.

So why are we linking our vision of our future self with a persona of an inner mentor? Let me try to answer with another question: Who would you pick as an outer (or actual human) mentor for yourself? It will likely be someone who has walked a journey that you would like to walk and is ahead of you. They have gathered invaluable experiences and will be able to tell you all about the challenges, learnings, milestones, etc. that you should be thinking about on your journey. The vision of your future self perfectly matches all these criteria! What better person could you find for this very important role of being your Inner Mentor?

Why Create an Inner Mentor?

By emphasizing the importance of an Inner Mentor voice and encouraging you to create one, I am, in no way, saying that outer mentors are not effective. They definitely are! In fact, they are a crucial part of your Hero's Journey.

But, your Inner Mentor can support you (or rather your brain) in ways that an outer mentor cannot. By tapping into the power of your own mind and imagination, you can make this future vision (your Inner Mentor) deeply familiar to your brain. This familiarity allows your brain to treat new external situations as though it has already encountered them, making them feel less daunting and more manageable. When our brain perceives these situations as familiar, we can bypass its natural resistance to change—its status quo bias—and overcome the fears that might otherwise hold us back from growth and expansion.

We can actually get playful with this, and start walking, talking, and living as if we were already in the shoes of our Inner Mentor. Doing so impacts our everyday being and the choices we make. Once you have the vision of your inner mentor firmly implanted in your mind, you can wake up every day and ask yourself, *"What would my Inner Mentor do? What would they wear and how would they walk and talk?"*

Your mentor is always going to be a more confident and wise version of yourself, as well as someone who is more relaxed with labels of success and failure. By asking yourself these questions and trying to act and think like your Inner Mentor, you're choosing to embody all the wisdom that you will eventually gain over time into your present day itself. And that will surely go a long way in helping you actualize the vision you have crafted of your future self.

The voice of your inner mentor can also be drawn upon when you find yourself at a crossroads in your life or career. If you're stuck between two options, you can ask what choice he/she would have needed to make when they faced a similar crossroad in order to get to their present place in life. It is just a brain hack that you are using, but one that can give you clarity and courage in the here and now, for the choices you need to make to move in the direction of your dreams.

Remember, however, that your future self is an evolving vision. None of us can actually have our lives turn out exactly the way we envision, nor can we fully become that version of our future self. And to be honest, that's not something you should be trying to achieve either! You simply need the direction and guidance that it offers so that you can keep growing into upgraded versions of yourself. The idea is not to become obsessed with matching this vision exactly, but to derive guidance, motivation and courage from it on a daily basis

Inner Child

The voice of the Inner Child is an inherent part of us. It can be thought of as just our own voice which is coming from another time. We grow out of that time but the thoughts, emotions, beliefs, grudges, dreams, etc. of the person we were back then stay alive within us. In fact, we have multiple voices of the Inner Child, each representing a different age of our childhood.

The more we can honor, integrate, and bring all these past versions of ourselves on board with one another and with our current way of thinking, the more coherence we will have in whatever we do. Thinking of it as trying to lead a flock of sheep. When there is coherence, they will all be moving in a streamlined direction toward a common destination. Without coherence, each one will want to go in the direction that they like best, thereby making it difficult (and often, impossible) to reach the destination.

Think back to the time when you first learned to drive a car. Your conscious mind was in complete attention back then and that was the one doing the work of driving. But, as you kept practicing and got more familiar with it, the knowledge of how to drive went deep into your subconscious mind too. As a result, your conscious mind might today be listening to a podcast/music, or looking out of the car window, or even talking to someone, but your subconscious mind is actually the one driving.

We faultily believe that our current adult mind is the one making all the decisions in our lives. What we do not take into account is that our subconscious mind typically has many versions of our Inner Child (be it a timid child or a rebellious teenager) - and any of them could be driving on a given day. One version might, metaphorically, hit the brakes and slow down whenever certain childhood fears get triggered. Or, another version might keep pushing the accelerator due to some strong aspirations that you felt back then. Everything that we learned or believed in as a child gets incorporated into our thinking when our Inner Child is in the driving seat, and that's how we land up behaving.

It's not like the Inner Child always, or even often, works against us. There are instances and situations when giving away the control of the driving seat to the child in us is beneficial and actually works for us. I can think of countless times that my Inner Child's voice has inspired me to do something fun or different, creating possibilities that my adult mind would not have done on its own.

The key is to remain aware of when your Inner Child's voice gets activated and then work consciously with it— sometimes you can let it inspire you and at other times you might need to negotiate with it.

<u>Exercise #2</u>

This exercise, which is divided into two parts, is for healing the wounds of your inner child and nurturing the joyful aspects of it. You want to get to the root of any fears, wounds, crushed dreams, or bad experiences that your Inner Child might have had and gently help him/her cope with them. Once the Inner Child is healed and whatever it was going through has been addressed, you may find yourself more likely to receive only the benefits that this voice brings. As more and more wounds from your past get healed, you will find that this voice will bring increasing joy, newness, and invigoration to your life!

Here are a few methods that you can use to heal and work with your Inner Child[9]. Like all the practices we have talked about so far, there will be one or two that work more effectively for you than the others. However, to identify that, I urge you to practice all the methods. Once you get familiar with a specific technique, use that whenever you feel that a certain situation has triggered your Inner Child.

1. Guided Imagery & Visualization: Use your imagination to create mental scenarios where you can meet and communicate with your Inner Child.

---

[9] If you feel ill equipped to try any of these techniques by yourself you can always seek the help of a licensed therapist. Most therapists will have experience in healing inner child wounds, although they might each have their own preferred methods.

2. Journaling & Letter Writing: Write letters to your Inner Child asking about his/her needs, desires, and fears.

3. Art Therapy: Tap into your Inner Child through creative outlets like drawing, painting, singing, or dancing.

4. Inner Child Dialogues: Actively engage in conversations (either aloud or in writing) with your Inner Child to better understand their thoughts and emotions.

The next part entails nurturing your Inner Child on an ongoing basis. Your work is not limited to healing the wounds of the Inner Child and developing a better relationship with her/her. You can take it a step further and actually begin to nurture the joyful, playful, and curious part of yourself. Studies have shown that aspects like creativity, divergent thinking, curiosity, and even the overall spark and zest for life that we have typically decreases with age. Thus, if you wish to retain these highly desirable traits in your life, your best bet is to do it through roping in your Inner Child—who already has these in abundance. Here are some ways to awaken him or her:

1. Participate in activities that you enjoyed as a child
2. Engage in imaginative play or role-playing games
3. Try new hobbies or activities that spark curiosity
4. Try creative pursuits like drawing, building, etc.

Inner Critic

This voice, as we know, manifests in different ways but gives the same outcomes. It limits us, makes us feel undeserving, judges our actions and decisions, makes us feel unsure about ourselves, and just pulls us down.

There are a few different approaches to dealing with this voice that you can choose from. Although, personally, I've noticed that the first step of simply gaining awareness also works wonders for me. When I can recognize my limiting thoughts as just being the voice of the Inner Critic, I separate myself from that voice and know that it is not the truth but rather just a distorted set of thoughts.

You can be rest assured that 95% of the time, the Inner Critic is not going to be useful for you. The Inner Critic voice mostly activates the reptilian brain, and we all know how useful (or not!) that is in terms of our advanced thinking and rational decision-making. And so, here's what I initially started doing when I felt this voice speaking up: If it started telling me, *"You could fail!"* I would write this down, take a deep breath, and then question myself as if I was a third person. I would ask myself varied questions that a coach might ask me - for example, whether failing would really be so disastrous in this situation.

If my calm and reasoned thinking affirmed that the failure might perhaps be too severe, I would choose to not go ahead with what I was planning to. This is to take care of the 5% of the times when the Inner Critic could actually protect us from making reckless moves. If, however, my calm and reasoned thinking told me that I could deal with the failure (should it happen) and that it's a risk I want to take, I would go ahead and do it.

When you initially start to tackle your inner critic, you can also use the above five step process of - pause, write, breathe (to switch out of your lizard brain), question/analyze, and then choose/act. As you get more used to recognizing and engaging with this voice, you will be able to do this on the go, and in a more intuitive way.

But at times when you decide to not follow the advice of your inner critic you will still need to deal with it in some way so that it does not keep hammering at you from within. This is a mental muscle and practice that you will eventually develop, and there are some tested techniques that you can experiment with as you eventually create the practices that will work best for you.

1. The first of these techniques circles back to the foundational step that we talked about with regard to dealing with this, and all the other voices. It uses pure awareness; simply notice the kind of mental chatter that goes on in specific situations, recognize it as the voice of the Inner Critic, and don't let it become significant to your decision-making. Just let it voice itself like an irrelevant radio in the background.

2. A second technique is to try empathizing with the motive of your Inner Critic, acknowledge it, and check whether it is relevant in your present. Many a times, when the voice warns us against doing something because we will get into trouble for it, it is basing it on something we have heard as children or some conditioning we may have received in the past. Hence, it is important to acknowledge where it is coming from and tell yourself (thereby telling your Inner Critic too) that those fears and inhibitions are not relevant in the here and now.

3. A third technique is to negotiate with the character of your Inner Critic. Here's an example of how this negotiation can go down: If the voice is discouraging you from attempting a project because it believes that you will lose money in it, strike a compromise and tell the voice (or the inner critic sitting inside of

you) that you will not put in all your money. If you do not listen or try to ignore it, your inner critic will keep nagging and nudging inside your head. Instead, listening to its concerns and finding a via media can help you create a quiet and coherent mind to move forward with the project.

4. There is another technique that I frequently rely upon as a follow up to technique 1. I try to anchor myself in my body through engaging in some mindful physical activity. And this is why it works: At the end of the day, the Inner Critic is a manifestation of our thoughts and a form of mental chatter. It is only in our mind, and not in our body or pure awareness. Hence, engaging in activities like running, dancing, yoga, deep breathing, etc. that gives us an escape from overthinking, lands up cutting off access from the Inner Critic as well.

5. One more brilliant technique that I have used with remarkable success is to call out the bluff of the Inner Critic. As we know, the inner critic is not a voice of truth but is based on beliefs that are subjective narratives and past inferences. So we can actually use our highest and most powerful truth at any moment to call out the lies of the inner critic. For this you can use any statement (an empowering one) that resonates deeply within you and that you personally regard as the truth. When you own this truth in the face of the lies, the lies will inevitably end up losing their hold. I often use the statement, *"I am the power and presence of God"*. You don't need to use the same statement—please experiment on your own and find a statement which resonates as TRUE for you.

It's important to recognize that our Inner Critic (along with its sub manifestations of Inner Jailor and Imposter syndrome) —will always be a part of us. Most of us will never be free of them completely, and that's okay. The key is not to silence these voices but to learn how to co-work with them in a harmonious, productive, and effective way. By doing so, you can prevent them from holding you back and instead use their presence to your advantage - giving you more clarity and confidence. Understanding and managing your inner dialogues better will allow you to take more courageous action steps in line with your dreams - and be less overwhelmed by doubt and fear.

Over time, you'll discover that engaging with your inner voices can open up new pathways to deep self-discovery and growth, touching not just your career but every area of your life. Letting the wisdom of your Inner Mentor guide your actions can propel you into new realities, transforming your state of being. Embracing and healing your Inner Child will bring creativity, passion, and authenticity into all you do. And by challenging—or even sidestepping—the judgments of your Inner Critic, you'll start to break free from self-imposed limitations, allowing you to pursue your aspirations with a renewed sense of freedom and determination.

This 3 part inner work is one of the key pillars to achieving the alchemic transformation that awaits you in terms of crafting, creating and steering your career. The more you can create coherence and alignment within all your inner voices, the more powerful, motivated, joyous, courageous, resilient and unstoppable you will become!

9

Leveraging Your Unique Weirdness

"What sets you apart can sometimes feel like a burden and it's not. And a lot of the time, it's what makes you great."

—Emma Stone

"Weird." It's a word that often carries a heavy, judgmental tone. "She's so weird!" or "He acted weirdly in that meeting!"—we've all heard these phrases, and let's be honest, they're rarely meant as compliments. Weird tends to signal something offbeat, something out of the ordinary—and more often than not, something undesirable.

But here's the thing: we've decided that's what weird means. Just like we've allowed societal definitions of words like success, work, and money to shape our thinking, we've done the same with 'weird.'

But what if we flipped the script? What if, by the end of this chapter, 'weird' became a word that no longer made you wince, but instead inspired you? What if weird simply meant different—and what if different was something worth celebrating? Imagine embracing your weirdness as a superpower, a unique set of qualities that sets you apart and allows you to bring something truly special to the table. My hope is that by the time you finish this chapter, you'll see being weird as a badge of honor, a signal that you're stepping into the fullness of who you are and transforming your career—and your life—by doing so.

Strength-Based Approach to Work

Let's begin this discussion with a fable.

In a faraway forest, all the animals came together to find a way to become wiser, better, and learn new things and grow. And hence, they decided to form a school. But simply forming a school was not enough, and they needed to zero in on what they would learn from the school too; i.e. a curriculum. So the animals came up with 6 core subjects- Running, Jumping, Flying, Climbing, Swimming, Crawling. The dog was excelling in the Running class, but when he attempted Climbing, it did not go as well, and he landed up with an injured leg. It took many days to heal and after that, even Running was not as easy or enjoyable for him as it once was. The duck thrived in the Swimming class but when she tried Running, it ended up wearing out the web of her feet and she lost her advantage in swimming too because it was painful. And so it went on ...

I hope you can see where I am getting at with this story, and how I am setting the foundation to explain the strength-based approach to work.

At the very start, some of you may be questioning how this story can be applicable since I am trying to get you to compare animals of different species with all of us humans who belong to the same species. And my answer is, though we belong to the same species, we are not all the same!

It is easier to explain the differences in animals because they have different physical features that give them differing capabilities. In humans instead, we have created concepts like strengths and weaknesses to explain what makes us unique and what capabilities we each bring to the table. Now, let me pose a question: What do you think is the correlation between your strengths, your performance in your career, and your happiness?

The good news is that these three are very closely related and if you choose wisely you will not have to trade-off between them. When you are playing to your strengths you will usually do well, and playing to your strengths will also make you happy. So these three things all move in tandem with each other. I'm telling you this based on research in organizational behaviour, but honestly, your own experience will give you the same inference as these studies.

Despite such clear evidence (both tangible and intangible) that points to the correlation between these three, we don't see too many people truly leveraging the power of their unique strengths at work in the best way it can be done. And this discrepancy is what we shall investigate further.

Notions of Ideal & The Competency Framework

One of the big reasons why doing something that we're good at does not always make us perform well or make us happy in our careers is due to the Notion of Ideal that we often get stuck with. It is a socially constructed notion and we hear it right from our early school days where one particular type of student gets labeled as the

'Ideal Student'. As we go on in our career journey, we get conditioned with how an 'Ideal Employee' or 'Ideal Manager' should be.

This construct of ideal is closely tied to the construct of roles. The reason behind defining roles (especially within organizations) is so that it becomes easier to find good personnel who can take up that role and get the work done. This is a pro, but it has its fair share of cons too.

The most important of which is that it limits people and their capabilities, and puts them into rigid boxes. It pits people against one another and often gives rise to unhealthy, unfair or ill-conceptualized comparisons. Comparing ourselves to anyone else is always like comparing apples to oranges, yet we mostly forget that it is only being done in the context of the role and we let it affect our overall self esteem.

Think back to the industrial age, when modern organizations and management as we know them first took shape. Strictly defined roles and competencies were essential back then. If people were allowed to innovate freely or step outside their rigid roles, it could have unravelled the entire organizational structure. Since changing roles wasn't an option, the solution was to change people—moulding them to fit the demands of their positions.

But times have changed. Today, with advancements in technology, communication, agile organizational structures, and flexible working norms, things have become much more fluid. Consider a small team of consultants: one might excel with numbers, another might shine in presentations, while a third is a natural at building client relationships. They can distribute the work in a way that plays to everyone's strengths. So, even if no single member embodies the 'Ideal Consultant,' the team thrives—and happiness follows suit.

This raises an important question: Is the competency framework many organizations rely on becoming outdated? In today's world, not everyone needs to master every skill listed for a particular role. You might excel in one area while lacking in another, but that's where a teammate's strength can fill the gap. This approach allows you to reshape your role to better fit your unique skills within the broader framework of the team.

In fact, even the research done on this topic maintains that if organizations want to retain their good performers, it is beneficial to let them play to their strengths. The organization gets to keep a high-performing employee and the employee gets to do something that they love and are good at. It's a perfect example of a win-win situation!

Now, I understand that for some of you, this strength-based approach to work might be feeling a bit uncomfortable. Perhaps you are wondering, *"What about my weaknesses? Is it not my job to fix them?"*

I'm not here to champion a purely strength-based approach that ignores your weaknesses altogether. What I'm advocating for is an informed choice—deciding how much you want to lean into your strengths and how much effort you want to put into developing your so-called weaknesses. The key is knowing that you have that choice. And here's the reassuring part: you can build a fulfilling and successful career no matter which path you choose.

Conformity & the Need to Fit In

This quest we have embarked upon—to embrace our true self and leverage our weirdness (because remember, being weird is good!) is more challenging than might appear on the surface. At the heart of this challenge lies our deep-rooted need to blend, agree and fit in with those around us. The pressure to conform is almost like having a background program running in our minds - constantly adjusting our thoughts and actions to align with that of the people around us.

From an early age, we're taught to seek approval and steer clear of rejection. The people we meet and the societal cues we pick up about what's "normal" shape our mental models about belonging vs being different. Over time, we start to mirror the majority, often pushing down our unique traits and individuality. This conditioning sets the stage for an internal conflict when we try to be our authentic selves. The deep-rooted urge to fit in can make us reluctant to share our true thoughts, feelings, and actions, worried about judgment or being left out.

To put it simply, conformity works like a prison. It interferes with our choices and clouds our perceptions. To break out of this prison however, we need to first understand how this subtle yet powerful prison operates. And that is what we are going to do next.

The Asch Experiments have been a classic breakthrough that proved that our brains indeed do not make decisions by themselves. They are continuously taking in information about how others are reacting or what they are voicing out about a certain situation or thing, and this information is integrated into our brain's own (supposedly independent) analysis.

Here's one of the simple early experiments done by Asch and his team. Person A (the subject of the experiment) was called into a room with some more participants, but unknown to A, the other participants were actually a part of the researcher's team. The tasks were very simple: Everyone had to give their answer aloud about which line from the right-side column most closely matched the line from the left-side column (see picture below).

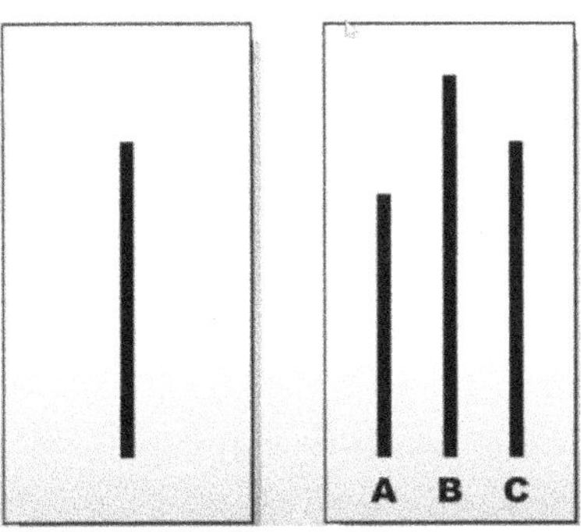

For one or two rounds, everyone gives the correct answer, which is line C in the example below. But, from the third round onwards, the stooges start systematically giving wrong answers. For example, the first person (who is in on the experiment) might say line A is the answer. Then the second does the same, and so does the third, and this cycle continues. Finally, comes the turn of Person A. Statistics showed that 37-38% of the time, the subject went along with the answer given by the group, even if it was wrong.

Come to think of it, do we not all do something similar while making choices in our own lives and careers? When our teenagers do it, we call it peer pressure. But I assure you, we adults are not exempt from it either. But how aware are we of the fact that we are changing our views and choices to match and mirror that of our peers? Are we doing this consciously or subconsciously? Asch and his team had the same question.

When they explored further to understand why the participants had conformed they identified two types of conformity.

The first type is informative conformity - when people actually believed that they were wrong and the rest of the group was right. These participants gave the majority answer because they truly started believing that it was the right answer. And this belief just came from the fact that others had claimed that to be the right answer.

The second type is normative conformity, when people believed that they were correct but went along with the group - just to fit in. They knew that the majority had the wrong answer, but they said it just because they do not want to stand out or seem different from the others.

I want you to pause and think about this a bit. Which type of conformity do you think we succumb to when we are making choices related to our careers? And which one is more dangerous, informational conformity (when our brain unconsciously follows the majority), or normative conformity (when we consciously prioritize fitting in over living our differences)?

In my experience as a career coach I have found that both these types of conformity are equally limiting, and both can hold us back from living and enjoying our full and unique potential. I myself had fallen prey to informational conformity, when I was doing my MBA, and started valuing the same jobs that everyone else around me valued. I had succumbed to normative conformity, in my early years as a faculty at IIMB when I had views that were different from my colleagues, but I did not speak my mind, because I really wanted to fit in with the rest.

Overcoming Our Brains Need to Conform

The good news is that the root antidote to overcoming both forms of conformity is courage! But different types of courage.

For overcoming normative conformity, it is the courage to be different. For overcoming informational conformity, it is the courage to make mistakes—to possibly be wrong or fail. Lets analyze the need for conformity from our brains perspective, and then we will be able to understand why we need these two different types of courage.

You see apart from the social conditioning that we have been subject to with respect to fitting in, there is also an evolutionary angle to conformity. It is as if our brains have a deep rooted need to fit in at any cost (sometimes even by overriding our own mind's truth).

Clearly, our brain believes that it is getting some benefits through conforming, and to convince our brain otherwise, we need to first understand those perceived.

Benefit 1 - Safety: Let's hop in a time machine and visit our caveman ancestors again. Just like the stress response that triggers Fight or Flight, the urge to conform was incredibly valuable back then, though it's more of a double-edged sword today. In those days, survival was all about being part of the group—a lone caveman didn't stand much chance on his own.

Further, if you were someone who stood out, guess what? You'd be the first to catch a predator's eye. So, blending in wasn't just about feeling comfortable—it was a survival tactic. Even as society advanced, there were steep consequences for not fitting in. Think about the term "outlaw"—someone literally cast out of society for not following the rules. Back then, laws weren't just legal codes; they were the fundamental principles of living together. Questioning those norms? That was a big no-no. Fitting in was crucial for enjoying the protection and perks of the group.

Benefit 2 - Group Identity: A huge part of who we are comes from the groups we belong to. Whether it's our nationality, gender, profession, or even family, these groups shape our identity. Our pride, self-esteem, and even our sense of status often come from these affiliations. So, when we refuse to conform or choose a different path from the group, it can feel like we're putting our very identity on the line. If everyone in the group is saying the same thing, it's tempting to just go along—not necessarily because we believe it, but to keep our place, our membership, and that comforting sense of belonging.

Benefit 3 - Wisdom of the Crowd: This idea suggests that large groups are often better than individual experts when it comes to solving problems, making decisions, or predicting outcomes. The logic is that while individuals can be biased, the collective knowledge of a crowd can smooth out those biases, giving a clearer and more accurate result.

Sounds pretty cool, right? Let's understand it with a simple example. Imagine a jar filled with pebbles, and everyone's asked to guess how many are inside. Some guesses will be spot-on, others way off. But if you average all the guesses, chances are it'll be really close to the actual number. That's the idea: while individual answers might miss the mark, the crowd's collective answer usually hits it.

But here's the million-dollar question: does this really work in every situation? Or are we losing our personal wisdom by blindly following the "wisdom of the crowd"?

Choosing a questioning approach

Here's the thing, each of these benefits of conformity - safety, group identity, and wisdom of the crowd, are all sometimes valid. However none of them are universally valid across all time periods, circumstances and problem types. But our brain does not realize that. The key to interrupt our brain's automatic tendency to conform is to keep asking questions. And the right kind of questions.

First, ask yourself whether it is a survival context for you. When I find myself at a crossroads of speaking my mind or just doing as everyone else is, here's what I tell myself: *"I am not a caveman! Even if I am not part of a herd and I don't fit in , my survival is not at stake."*

Second, think about your group identities. How important are they to you, psychologically and emotionally? Ask yourself, *"If I am not part of this group, would I still be happy to just be me?"* I hope your answer is a big, confident "Yes!" every time.

Third, question the relevance of crowd wisdom for the situation at hand. Trusting the average only works when the crowd has the same data, and everyone is equally skilled and knowledgeable about the problem—like in the pebble experiment. But when it comes to personal, subjective decisions—like your career choices—asking more people doesn't necessarily bring you closer to the "right" answer, *because there isn't one*! Each person sees the world through their own lens, which might not match yours.

Alongside the above three questions you can also ask yourself whether it is a context in which you can afford to make mistakes. Revisiting our discussion about the Fear of Failure, don't let just the remote possibility of something going wrong prevent you from attempting it in the first place. Talk to yourself about how big or significant the potential mistake can be. If it feels like something that you can handle, don't let the possibility of making mistakes hold you back.

Lastly, try to understand why others around you are behaving in a particular way. And once you identify their reasons, check in with yourself about whether those specific reasons and priorities are valid and relevant to you. If they are not, you can definitely give yourself (and your brain) the permission to break free and walk on your unique and different path, one that is right just for YOU!

I'd like to clarify something rather important here before we close this section. I'm not advocating non-conformity just for the sake of it. I'm not trying to turn you all into rebels. There are times when the wisdom or viewpoints of the majority might actually make sense and staying within a group is beneficial for us. It is up to us to mindfully identify these times and that is where the questioning approach outlined above can really help.

Wrongness to Strongness Approach

The name of this section is a bit of a giveaway, and I'm guessing you already have a bit of an idea about what it entails. And along with that idea, you perhaps have skepticism about it too because after all, how can something wrong in us be our strength? And the deeper question here is, should it be?

I want you to think about a hurricane. Try to visualize it; the power, the speed, and the intensity. You may have also visualized the destruction it typically leaves behind. And thinking about that would make you categorize it as a bad thing because it disrupts our lives. But, if you look at it by itself, it is just a force, an intense strongness.

Right from our childhood, there are often things that we are made wrong for. Speaking from personal experience, I've been made wrong for things like being a chatterbox, asking too many questions, and being restless. I remember an incident wherein one of my mother's friends had come as a substitute teacher to my school and her feedback to my mother had been, *"Your daughter disrupted the class! She kept asking irrelevant questions."*

In my mind, those questions did not feel irrelevant, and I did it with no intention other than to satisfy my curiosity. But I got a yelling for it. Perhaps the voice of my Inner Child still feels the sting of it, but I can now take control of the narrative and tell myself that thinking out of the box, is actually one of my superpowers.

It's your turn now. Reflect on all the things you were shamed for, made to feel guilty about, or scolded for as a child. Now, look at those very things through a new lens: Perhaps you were made to feel wrong about those things because that particular quality in you was too strong for adults around you to handle. Or perhaps it disrupted their reality in some way, or it made them feel scared for your safety or ability to fit in.

With this new perspective, you can now form a better relationship with those inherent qualities that you might have shunned (or suppressed) because you never got positive responses for them as a child. And some of these qualities might very well turn out to be your superpowers—which you can now leverage going forward. Remember, if that quality was so strong that it got noticed and singled out for you to get a scolding, you must have been quite an outlier in it. And you now have an opportunity to convert that 'wrongness' that you were made to believe you possess into a strongness.

There is an incredible lightness and healing that you will experience as you revisit those supposedly 'bad' parts of yours with a lens of non-judgment. Give yourself the permission to see and own the pure potency or raw quality that fuelled the so-called 'bad behaviour' in your childhood.

Let's revisit the comparison with the hurricane and the havoc that it can wreck. Some of your qualities too might have led you to hurt someone or act out in a way that was dangerous or disruptive for yourself or others. But always remember that the only wrong thing back then was how or when you expressed that quality, and not the quality itself. Acknowledge the times when it did not work well for you and others, because it will keep you grounded and mindful about how you can use it in the future.

As you craft your career look for ways to nurture these once 'blacklisted' qualities and use them in a positive way. Just like I have channelled my 'wrongness' of being a 'chatterbox' into an asset as a professor and speaker, and my 'wrongness' of asking 'irrelevant questions' into becoming an innovator in the field of education.

Your Unique Tree of Life

We are now going to use the metaphor of a tree to depict all your unique strengths and values in one place. Like any tree we see in nature, this tree that will represent you will also have two distinct parts. There are the roots, which grow beneath the soil and quietly support it without being seen. And then there are the gorgeous branches which visibly remain in front of our sights always. When we think about trees, it is this part that is above the ground that first comes to our mind. But, can the tree even be in existence without the roots that we often fail to think about? No!

The roots are, in fact, the reason why the tree flourishes and because of which we can see and enjoy the gifts of the branches, leaves, and flowers. The roots have a tough journey in front of them. Through the darkness, dampness, and resistance, they have to grow and support the tree. This is a critical part of the tree's journey that is not known or visible to others, nor glamorous in any way.

While creating your sketch for this exercise, start with the roots—which you will label as the things that are deeply important and non-negotiable for you—your core values. You have already identified them in chapter 3, so you can just pick them out from your earlier notes. Like the roots of a real tree also absorb nourishment from the soil, think about how your values are also giving you stability and nourishing your personality in unique ways.

Coming to the branches, depict these as your strengths, all the gifts and talents that you possess. Think of all your past accomplishments that have made you proud and reflect on what strengths you must have possessed (*which you still do!*) that made those accomplishments possible. Next, think about the things that people compliment you for doing so easily, because those will also point to your strengths. And last but not the least, revisit the qualities that you earlier thought of as a wrongness, (identify the underlying potency) that made that wrongness possible and boldly claim that now as a strength.

The way I like to think of this tree is that the roots depict the unique essence of who we are 'Being', while the branches depict the unique qualities that aid in our 'Doing'. The world only gets to see our Doing (branches, flowers and fruits), and yet in order to keep doing, we need to strengthen and nourish our 'Being'. At the end of the day we are Human Beings, not just Human Doings.

Your Unique Treasure Chest

For this section, I want you to start looking at anything else that you may already have that can help you in your career. Think of all your degrees, certifications, awards, recognitions, qualifications and past positions. You can also include your personal brand or social reputation as well as your wealth, savings, properties and other tangible resources. In this chest you are acknowledging all your resources and aids accumulated over the years—basically anything that you can choose to use and leverage or build on, as you craft future career possibilities for yourself.

At one point of time, I had started thinking of some of my college degrees as burdens because I was not using them. It took me a while, but I have now realized that anything can be an asset— should I choose to see it as one. For example, even though my engineering knowledge is now not useful for the work I do, I realized that my IIT degree opens doors to many software organizations and technical audiences who are willing to put their trust in me because of it.

Here's another example. One of my coaching clients had inherited multiple properties which she thought were not related to her career - but after acknowledging it as part of her treasure chest she found a way to leverage one of them as a therapy centre in a business she co-founded with someone she met.

And so, don't leave out mentioning something in your treasure chest just because you think it is not a direct asset to your career right now. It might have untapped potential to be a resource or support for you, possibly in an indirect manner or in combination with a future opportunity that is yet to come your way.

Your Unique Network of Co-Creators

Here's a thumb rule of having a successful career that I have come to understand over the years: While the things that you know and that you're good at matter, the people you know and who you're connected to matter equally, if not more. Your network can open doors, offer opportunities, spark new ideas, create collaborative possibilities and help you and your career in so many other ways. And do not forget, it can also be an excellent source of outer resilience.

So the absolutely unique set of people who you know and are already connected to is an opportunity in itself that is waiting to be leveraged! But before you can get to the stage of leveraging it, you must acknowledge that you have it and recognize that it is a blessing and asset in your life. And that is why I encourage you to list your key connections (or groups of connections like alumni groups) all in one list.

Exercise 1 - Drawing your Tree of Life & Resources

Take your time to do this exercise. Remember that there is no right or wrong way to do it. What works best for most people is to go through at least 3 iterations of drawing— adding or modifying what feels intuitive and authentic to you each time.

Remember that this exercise is best done as a combination of using your right and left brains. Allow your left brain to list and give you points to include and allow your right brain to guide you to insert / draw, group and label the points at the right places. Allow your right brain to help you decide the height, length, width and depth of roots, number of branches etc., and also the form of the tree , kinds of leaves, fruits and flowers you might want to include optionally. This is your TREE. You get to draw it in a way that feels nurturing, soulful, and inspiring for you.

Use colours, use your imagination and tap into your playful creative self. Most people typically find it rewarding to create their tree of life on paper. However, some people like to create it as a PowerPoint slide or some other form of digital art. You can experiment with both and see which works better for you.

Be creative and find space to include your treasure chest & network of co-creators on the same sheet of paper (or digital page) where you create your tree of life. The reason to put it all down on one page is so that when you look at it, you can allow your brain to just gaze over all the points in one go and come up with creative ideas, combinations, and possibilities related to crafting your career forward[10].

Be sure to put your drawing up at a place where you can see it regularly and be reminded of it. We often forget or fail to harness all the things we have been gifted with, already have available or what we have worked hard to acquire. By reinforcing your unique values, strengths, abundant resources and network of people, your brain will feel a renewed sense of confidence and motivation each time your eyes fall on this picture.

Your brain will also get new ideas of ways to use underutilized strengths or combine them with other resources. Finally, each time you see this drawing, it will be a reminder that it is your responsibility to look after, protect, and nurture this tree so that it can thrive, grow, fruit and flower and be a contribution to this world. These three by themselves are good enough reasons to make this drawing. However, I am going to give you one more way in which you can leverage the drawing once you have made it—and that is to develop your USP!

Developing your Unique Selling Proposition (USP)

In the world of marketing, a Unique Selling Proposition (USP) refers to the distinct factor that makes a product or service stand out from its competitors. This concept is equally (if not more) important in a career context, where a USP represents the unique combination of skills, experiences, qualities and values that will

---

[10] This will also be useful to you for the effectuation approach that we will discuss in chapter 10

differentiate you in the job market, or as a service provider if you are freelancing on your own (as I am).

Think of it basically as the essence of what makes you interesting and valuable (to employers or clients), setting you apart from others in your field, and making you un-substitutable by anyone else. And as you grow in your career your USP will also be what allows you to set and negotiate your own salary (or service charges).

See this is the flip side of the pain of not fitting in. We can turn it into the privilege of being special and irreplaceable.

So how can you develop your USP (and make sure it remains unique)? By capitalizing on your weirdness! Your difference! and definitely those qualities where you were anyways so off the charts that you got singled out and scolded for as a child.

You have already laid the foundation by creating your tree of life and listing your values, strengths, qualities, resources, and connections. As you look over this page that you have created, remind yourself that nobody else on this planet will have exactly that same combination of all the elements that you have. So in a very wide sense - this tree itself becomes your USP. However, as you journey through your career, depending on the specific job / role, or service that you are providing at any point in time you can create a USP for that role or service by looking back to your tree of life and extracting a subset of strengths relevant to the context or job.

One of the reasons many people fail to create a USP in their careers is because they have not done the inner work of understanding how to move their brain beyond its default tendency to conform. Their brain will keep nudging them towards being like everyone else, betting that it is the safer option. However, you now know how to move beyond the trap of conformity and allow yourself to stand out differently with your unique gift-set of qualities, values and strengths.

The second reason people fail to create their USP is that they themselves have not yet let go of the judgment of being different, or are worried about being viewed as weird by others. When you stand in your differences, some people might see you for the gift that you are, but there is also a risk that some others might judge you.

What you have to make peace with is that you don't have any control over other people's judgments. What you can let go of however, is you judging yourself for being different. And once you have your own back on this just focus your energies on using your difference to make a stellar contribution through your work. Usually, when your contribution shines through, then even the naysayers will slowly begin to accept your different way of being and doing.

So brace yourself to ignore any judgment that might come your way from others, embrace your weirdness, craft an un-substitutable USP and go rock the world! It is your hero's journey after all—not anyone else's! And guess what, the world needs you to be 'YOU', to make your best contribution to others. You can be a top class version of yourself but only a mediocre version of someone or something that is not truly you.

10

Using Goals: A Double Edged Tool

"By recording your dreams and goals on paper, you set in motion the process of becoming the person you most want to be. Put your future in good hands — your own."

Mark Victor Hansen

The concept of 'setting goals' or 'working toward' goals has gained a lot of traction in the recent years. The usage of this word has also become very common, not only in terms of one's career but also in our personal lives.

But before we join this race of setting and pursuing goals, let's pause to understand the fundamentals first. Because you may just decide that you don't want to be a participant in this race at all, and that's completely fine!

I've been teaching a course that focuses on this concept of goals for many years now. And in every batch, there is a question that I invariably get asked- *"Do we have to have goals?"* And my answer is no; there is no compulsion of any kind to have goals. If you think about it on a deeper level, goals are just another societal construct that we humans have created, and which we use to bring about order and motivation in our lives and careers. Goals do not exist in nature. And it is very much possible to live a fruitful, and rewarding life without having goals as well.

That being said, goals can also be an extremely effective tool, as has been the case with me. They have helped me immensely in achieving things which I absolutely would not have otherwise[11].

But it remains a tool of choice—even for me!

And in case you make the choice of leveraging this tool, I want to help you do it in an informed manner so that you can get the best results from it. Think of tools like knives or hammers; they are useful but they come with their own set of dangers. Goal setting is also like a double-edged sword. I want to help you leverage the functional and beneficial aspects of using goals and make you aware of the downsides that can accompany it, so you can minimize the chances of hurting yourself.

At the outset, let's revisit the concept of Value Coherence because this is going to be crucial for you to be able to derive sustainable benefits through using the process of goal setting. Let's go back to the discussion we had about redefining success and work, and how important it was to craft these terms in a way that stuck true to your values. All these concepts are deeply interconnected in your inner experience of your career. Just as your notions of success and work should align with your core values, so too must your goals.

When your goals are in coherence with your values (the things that you hold close and sacred to your heart), you will feel an inner power that makes the journey of setting and achieving those goals much easier. But if your goals and values pull you in different directions, you will constantly be torn between two sides and will dissipate your energy in trying to overcome your own inner conflict each time you sit down to work.

---

[11] Like my childhood story I shared in Chapter 3 about how I put up alphabets of IIT on my wall. That was goal setting in its rawest form.

So whatever specific goals you decide to set for yourself in your career and life, make sure to align these with your core values (think back to whatever you have put down as the roots of your Tree of Life). Remember always, that your roots symbolize what is essential and non-negotiable for you to grow, thrive and deliver in a sustained manner.

Effects of Goal Setting

Each of our actions and choices comes with its own consequences. If you decide to start leveraging goals to help in your work and life, some effects are bound to follow—you can be sure of that! However, the effects that we will discuss here may not manifest in the same way for everyone. It is not even necessary that all these effects will occur for you every time and with every goal you set. Think of these more as the superset of effects that can occur when you use the tool of goal setting.

As we explore these eight effects, take time to reflect on and verify them against your own experiences. Even though you may have never looked at the concept of goal setting in as nuanced a manner as we now will, I am sure each of you has at least dabbled in it. And hence, you will have a fair idea of how it worked for you, what it did for you, and how it made you feel.

If you remember the story about 'Good thing, bad thing, Who knows?', we discussed that our brains never really have the complete information to categorize anything as good or bad. We end up prematurely labelling things and limiting ourselves to a very specific perception of them. However, there is a broad categorization that we can make in terms of classifying these effects as 'mostly desirable' or 'mostly undesirable', based on the way they typically work.

Some of the more desirable effects of goal setting include setting a direction to our life, or creating a sense of meaning and purpose for us. But there are undesirable ones too like triggering behavior that is incoherent with our sense of ethics or limiting our possibilities.

Let us look at these effects in detail. And then, I leave it up to you to decide which effects work for you and which work against you, based on what you choose to create through your goal setting adventures.

1. Help with Navigation

Goal setting helps us navigate our lives and careers and sets a direction. To understand this better, think of an airplane. It has a certain destination (a certain goal) that it needs to get to, but if you look at the route that it takes, the nose of the airplane is not always pointing toward where it has to eventually land. Yet, even though it goes up and down, and swerves left and right, it will eventually reach its chosen destination.

That's the similar kind of journey that our lives and careers also follow! Having clear goals helps us navigate all sorts of challenges and crossroads. Just like the nose of the airplane, we may go through different routes and chase different paths, but having set goals will always make us come back and re-navigate toward where we dream of going.

2. Increase in Focus

Having goals increases our focus on whatever it is we are doing and helps with minimizing distractions. Its function can be compared with that of the side-blinders used on racehorses; it allows them to see nothing more or less than what they need to focus on. Now, this of course comes with its own disadvantages, something that we will address later in effect 8. But for now, let's talk about how this can be a helpful thing as well.

We humans are naturally curious and creative beings, constantly drawn to the myriad of things happening around us. This trait is often associated with children who are easily distracted and have a short attention span. However, as adults, we too can be sidetracked by countless distractions. However, when we set a certain goal, our own brain's bounded awareness (which we learnt about in Ch 1) begins to work like the side blinders of a race horse. And even when some things do manage to catch our attention and tempt us, seeing that ending line of our goal helps us to zone in, keep our head down, and just get the work done.

3. Neural Hack of Urgency

Our brains are like gadgets that come with certain pre-set algorithms and functions. Some of them, like the intricate stress response system, were designed in a way that helped the survival of our ancestors. They may not be functional for us today, but they once had a very important purpose to serve.

Another one of these inbuilt algorithms is that our brains will always prioritize something that is urgent over something that is important.

Think of a 2x2 matrix, wherein you have urgency on one axis and importance on the other. Every activity that we undertake can be grouped into the 4 categories that can be formed using this matrix. The top-right corner will have the high urgency and high importance tasks whereas the bottom-left corner will have the low urgency and low importance tasks. There's a very clear distinction that our brains make between these two categories. The former will always be prioritized over the latter.

But where our brain starts working against us is when it needs to decide between tasks that fall in the remaining categories of this matrix, i.e. when it has to choose between low urgency high importance tasks or high urgency low importance tasks. For most people, the first category might include things like working on long-term projects, personal development, upskilling, exercising, etc.

The second category typically has things like replying to emails and messages, making necessary phone calls, time bound chores etc. And because of the inherent wiring of our brain, it is always going to prioritize the second category over the first one. As a result the things that are actually important for us (but not urgent) keep getting postponed, while our days get filled up with urgent but not important activities.

The trick to combat this unhelpful wiring of our brains is to deliberately convert something that is not urgent into something that is very urgent. And the easiest way to do this, is to set goals with specific deadlines.

When I was doing my PhD, this is the trick I used on my own brain. I was running the risk of delaying my completion, because my dissertation was a long term (and open ended) project compared to so many other things that required my urgent attention on a daily basis. It could have theoretically gone on forever. So I set myself a firm goal of finishing it by a certain date, and I put up that date on my desk and in my office. There was no pressure put on me by anyone outside, but just seeing that date every day created a simulated sense of urgency for my brain -and that's how I finished my PhD in the time that I had set for myself.

4. Create Meaning and Purpose

Setting goals is a very powerful way to give us a sense of meaning and purpose. In chapter 7, we have already covered how impactful this is in helping us developing our inner resilience.

When you feel ignited by a sense of purpose, you literally become a superhuman version of yourself. This is evident in almost every domain, be it the corporate world, social sector, education, politics or even parenting. Goals very naturally give us that sense of purpose that makes us want to get up each day, get things done, and just keep going.

This works on an individual as well as group level. A shared sense of purpose gives a wonderful kind of energy to the entire group and also creates a strong sense of bonding. A common goal, can also give a group a shared identity, where there might have been none before, and with this shared identity comes motivation and drive and purposeful action.

5. Fuel Anxiety and Fear of Failure

Undoubtedly, goal setting increases our concentration and motivation to get things. But it can also land up fuelling our anxiety in the process.

Revisiting the example of my PhD, nobody had really asked me to set that strict deadline by which I had to complete it. It was something that I imposed upon myself, a goal that I myself set, and it still created a fair degree of anxiety for me. Having that constant ticking clock and realizing that I was yet far away from the finish would send my brain into a mild panic on a daily basis.

Setting goals can also introduce a "fear of failure" where none existed before. By establishing a fixed target, we inadvertently create benchmarks for success and failure. This means that the act of setting a goal can turn what was once just a 'do your best task' into a situation where we might succeed or fail, depending on whether or not we reach that target.

6. Trigger Unethical Behaviour

Surprising as it might seem, goals can trigger unethical behavior in us, especially when we are strongly attached to the outcome we desire. How, you might ask, does this happen? When we end up making our goals very important for us we trap our brains into a paradigm of compulsion. Our mental chatter becomes something along the lines of, *"I have to achieve this!"* We create an internal sense of urgency and desperation inside our brains. And we already know that when we feel desperate in any situation, our stress response is triggered. We slip into the Flight or Fight mode and start thinking from our reptilian brain. And our reptilian brain is not inherently the most ethical part of our minds—it will think in black and white, focusing only on what it needs in the moment.

You might normally function with a strong set of principles, ethics, and values guiding you. This is when your frontal lobes are in control of your choices and decision making. However, when your reptilian brain has hijacked your thinking, your brain's choice algorithm becomes something way more basic and savage, and we run the risk of not abiding by our values and ethics.

This again reinforces the importance of creating value coherent goals, because if your goals naturally make you tread the path of your values, you will be less likely to stray from it even during your goal pursuit journey.

7. Induce Low Self Esteem

Setting goals can also induce low self-esteem and leave us feeling like we're not enough. You see, our self-esteem, our internal belief of how good we are is continuously at risk due to many factors. People and events around us often make us feel like we're not good enough. It's like we feel a constant pressure to keep doing things to prove to ourselves that we're good at the things we do and the various roles we essay in our lives.

When we set goals, we are, in a way, adding to this onslaught of pressure and reinforcing the belief that we are not good enough 'yet'. Our goals are always going to be at a point higher or farther than where we are right now, because they are always going to be about something better that we want to achieve. So when we compare the end point of our goals to where we currently are, it serves as a cruel reminder of how far back we are and how much more work we have to do.

These nagging thoughts can make us feel unworthy, like we will never be good enough to make it up to our goals, and such downward spiralling mental chatter eventually lands up lowering our self-esteem.

In my experience as a coach I have yet to come across a person who does not suffer from some variation of the 'I'm not enough' disease that is so widespread today. And the goals we set might just land up increasing the intensity of this disease.

8. Limit Possibilities

As a flipside to the benefit of enhancing our concentration, goals can also end up restricting our options and possibilities.

Let's go back to the discussion about Bounded Awareness - our mental lens that filters the infinite data inputs we can get from our surroundings and lets us focus on only those that are most relevant to us at any given moment. Goal setting is one way to intentionally manipulate our own bounded awareness (or that of other people).

Setting goals can indeed improve our concentration and help us work more efficiently towards a desired target. However, this focus can also cause us to miss out on other valuable opportunities. For example, if a person works with a singular focus toward getting a promotion in their current job, they might overlook a fantastic opportunity elsewhere because their awareness is completely absorbed by their current goal.

If you go back and think about your own experiences with goal setting and reflect on the above eight effects described above, you might find that the first four effects have mostly worked to your advantage, while the last four have not. So is this always going to be a trade-off situation for us? Or is there a way we can stand to gain the advantages of goal setting and minimize the costs associated with it?

And that is what we shall explore next through an example of climbing a mountain!

Two Ways of Climbing a Mountain

Imagine a mountain climber, who can choose to complete his task in one out of two ways. Both these have the same target of getting to the peak, and so both are using goals. But let's see how and why they differ, and which one is in the mountain climber's best interests.

In the first method (which we can refer to as Method A), the mental chatter and the things that the mountain climber keeps telling himself are, *"It's really important for me to reach the peak. When I reach the peak, I will have succeeded - only then I will be good enough. I have to reach it at any cost, and when I finally reach it, then I will be happy."*

In the second method (Method B), however, the chatter takes on a very different form. The mountain climber tells himself things like, *"I'd love to reach that target. But I am also going to invest in the journey and enjoy it. I am curious about what new things I can learn and discover along this route. And I am happy right now, in the experience of this moment."*

As so, as he climbs up every day, he stops to look back at how far he has come. He celebrates and savours his progress and the small victories. He enjoys the beauty of nature, and makes friends with his co-travellers and the people he meets on the way. He gets curious about the new things he sees and keeps learning more about himself, his peers, and his surroundings. He makes sure that he shows up each day and does his very best towards reaching the goal. He is present and happy in the 'now', and not dependent on a future 'win' to make him happy.

And now, let's revisit the list of the eight effects of goal setting that we discussed earlier in the context of these two ways of climbing the mountain. This is to help you understand how you too can choose something along the lines of approach B and leverage the beneficial outcomes of goal setting while building defences against the potentially harmful ones.

Both methods provide a clear direction to guide the mountain climber toward the summit, no matter where she is on her journey (effect 1). So the benefits of navigation can be reaped equally whether you follow approach A or approach B. Same is the case with the benefit of creating meaning and purpose (effect 4). Both approaches will yield this equally.

Both methods also provide increased concentration (effect 2), though we must remember that while increased focus offers benefits, it also has the downside of limiting possibilities (effect 8). These two effects will typically trade-off against one another and they need to be balanced effectively. There is a subtle mindset hack however that you can use to hold your end goal in focus and also stay open to possibilities.

The key to do this is through embodying a Beginner's Mindset, which is part of approach B. Yes, the goal and target is very important and it needs our focus to get there. But, we should also not give up on our inherent sense of curiosity. With the curiosity of a Beginner's Mind, the climber will still notice interesting or different things along his journey, and will be able to give himself the space and opportunity to explore those without losing sight of the peak (as target). Depending on the situation the climber may even decide to either explore or not explore the other things she spots. What is important is that she was able to spot these other opportunities and possibilities, and then make an informed choice about whether to engage with them or not.

In both methods, A & B, goals can act as a brain hack, creating a false sense of urgency (effect 3). However, Method B adds an extra element: *Present Moment Awareness.* This awareness helps you manage and balance that urgency, providing a way to regain your focus when things become overwhelming.

While a sense of urgency can drive us to accomplish tasks, it should not dominate our minds or lead to excessive stress. Present Moment Awareness serves as a counterbalance, grounding and stabilizing us. It also can serve as a gateway to experience a flow state in whatever task we might be doing—something we saw in chapter 4, when discussing different ways of reverse engineering the flow state.

Next, let's compare both methods in terms of how goals fuel anxiety (effect 5). Say, the mountain climber has given himself 15 days to reach the summit, and it is already day 10 and he is behind his predicted schedule. In which of the two methods do you think he is going to be more afraid of failure and more likely to get anxious?

Method A associates success and accomplishment only with reaching the summit. But Method B also counts the experience, learning, and wisdom along the journey to the summit. And so, even if he happens to fail in his ultimate goal, under Method B, there will always be the consolation that all those efforts have given back something in the bargain. But that won't be the case in Method A, - which makes it much more likely for the climber to experience a greater fear of failure and much higher levels of anxiety.

To examine the triggering of unethical behavior (effect 6), let's add a situation to the story of the mountain climber. Say, another climber has been injured along the path and the only way to go ahead is to just ignore this person or even perhaps step over him. The odds of the climber choosing to do so is higher in Method A. And that's because in Method B, all the stakes are not attached to the outcome and so there's less desperation to go against our personal values or sense of ethics. Moreover in Method B, control has not been hijacked by our reptilian brain and we will be able to analyze the complexities of the situation with our whole brain.

And finally, let's examine the risk of goals lowering our self-esteem (effect 7). In Method A, the climber has repeatedly told himself that he will be good enough only once he reaches the summit. So along the entire journey, the climber will always feel like something is lacking in him. And God forbid, if he cannot make the peak, he will never feel worthy enough because he had linked his self worth to the completion of his goal.

However, in Method B, there's a sense of acknowledging and celebrating everything that the climber has seen or done so far, and that helps to keep up the self-esteem. Because of the learning mindset the climber's self-esteem can even increase if she chooses to count what she has learnt or how she has grown in the process. The thinking becomes that while it will be great to reach the summit, she will still be ok and good enough even if she does not get there this time. Inbuilt into approach B, are facets of internal resilience which we covered in chapter 7.

Antidotes to the Traps of Goal Setting

The benefits and ill effects of goal setting do not ask for our permission before making their way into our minds. It is something that just happens! While it is wonderful to be more driven, focussed, and work singularly toward a good cause, we do not want to feel overly limited or stressed due to our goals. So we want to lean more towards approach B , rather than approach A when striving towards the goals and targets that we set for ourselves.

But how can we tackle something like our inherent mental chatter that catches us unaware? Think back to the approach we took while working with our inner voices. We knew that they would invariably come up in our minds and so, trying to run away from them was not the solution. Instead, we used some measures to try to manage and nurture them in a way that would benefit us.

Similarly, we can use some guidelines to ensure that even if the unfavorable effects of goal setting find their way toward us, we cope with them in a healthy manner and try to limit the impact they have on us. We can do these in parallel with our goal setting.

You might have already picked up a few ideas such as savouring the journey, celebrating your wins along the way, developing a Beginner's Mindset and keeping your curiosity alive through our analysis of the mountain climber's story.

Here is a specific checklist that you can use to dodge the traps that goal setting may lay for you:

1. Cultivate a sense of non-judgmental self acceptance toward yourself. Practice an internal narrative that is something like, *"Whether I achieve my set goals or not, I am always good enough! My self worth is independent of what I achieve externally."*

2. Acknowledge the Gain, and not just the Gap. Instead of focusing only on the things you have yet to achieve or the things you still need to do in pursuit of your goals, also appreciate and

count everything that you have already done. The ways in which you have grown and become better, and the experience that you have gained so far. Build up momentum for your next day, through listing and celebrating the progress you have made today (this is part of something known as the Progress Principle in management).

3. Rejoice in the efforts (even if they seem small and insignificant) that you are taking toward fulfilling your goals. Invest in the process and consciously savour and enjoy the journey of action, learning and growth. Celebrate yourself for just showing up with a heroic mindset, each day and each moment. Let your happiness be derived from your experience of working, and not be contingent on the achievement of the final outcome.

4. Ground yourself, again and again and again—in present moment awareness. Your goal is not real, it is a fictional creation in your mind related to the future. The future itself exists only in your mind. The only real thing you have is your present moment. It is the only place where we have any real power, and where we actually can take action. So even as you use this fictional construct of a goal as a tool and brain hack, remember that your reality, *your truth and your power lies only in the present moment.* So make sure you have a way to keep coming back to it.

5. Finally, develop the willingness to let go. We set goals to fulfil a certain craving or a desire. We set goals because we would like to do something, create something, or achieve something. But, there's always a very real possibility that despite our best efforts, we may not succeed in fulfilling that desire. And that's where *learning to let go* can prove very beneficial to us. The practice of letting go also

allows us to stay flexible and open to new alternatives. Also, if we ever need to pivot or reset our goals, our sense of self is not so tightly bound to the earlier goal that we risk losing ourselves with it.

The most important thing is to always remember that you have chosen to include goals as tools to aid with direction, focus, motivation, and a sense of purpose. You are ultimately using goals for the objective of making yourself better, more accomplished, or happier. *Don't ever let them become bigger than you!* In an inner sovereignty approach, YOU are always the master who can choose to use, change, or even drop a tool when it is not working for you.

Not all Goals Work Alike on our Inner World

All goals that we set, be it in our careers or personal lives, are similar in their eventual purpose, which is to give us a set direction or target to work toward. But the way different types of goals do this, and how they influence our thinking and emotions differs. I'm going to introduce you to three facets to look out for as you craft goals for yourself. Once you understand why each of these is important, you can then make informed decisions about which type will work the best for you and which you want to avoid—*situation by situation.*

1. Intrinsic & Extrinsic Goals

The former category are goals that you create for yourself because you want to. The latter, however, covers the goals that your boss, your parents, your mentors, or society at large sets for you.

The mentality towards achieving extrinsic goals becomes one of obligation—you have to do it because you've been told to. Intrinsic goals, however, stem from your own choices and desires, and hence, they have much more power to inspire and motivate you in your journey. With extrinsic goals, unless you are completely aligned with them internally and resonate deeply with them, you are likely to experience resisting emotions because it feels like someone else is controlling you and making you do things.

In my own crafting journey, (and also when I work with clients), I prioritise intrinsic goals because they are more effective, not only in terms of creating results but also in terms of experiencing happiness along the journey of goal striving (the journey that we undertake to attain our goals).

2. Approach & Avoidance Goals

Approach goals and avoidance goals represent two distinct motivational orientations. Approach goals focus on achieving positive outcomes, such as acquiring new skills, earning a promotion, or improving relationships. These goals are driven by the desire to attain something beneficial or rewarding. In contrast, avoidance goals are centered around preventing negative outcomes, such as avoiding failure, criticism, or loss. These goals are motivated by the desire to steer clear of undesirable situations or consequences.

While avoidance goals do give you motivation and momentum, the energy of *"I don't want this!"* is not an uplifting or inspiring feeling. There's often no sense of deeper meaning or purpose linked to such goals either, and they simply work as an escape route. .

What I recommend is to try and create approach goals whenever possible. Wherever you find yourself creating avoidance goals (out of old habit), sit down, reflect and convert it consciously into an approach goal instead. For example, instead of the avoidance goal "Don't get overlooked by potential clients," you can come up with an approach goal like "Build a strong personal brand to attract new clients." Instead of having the avoidance goal, "Avoid working late into the evening," you could set an approach goal such as, "Establish a healthy work schedule that allows time for relaxation and personal activities each day."

Converting an avoidance goal into a related approach goal is not simply a play of words. It gets your brain to actually start thinking about what you would like in the future instead of whining about what you do not want. *It shifts your focus, mindset, and yes your energy too!* Most importantly, it sets you up for success by allowing your brain to leverage the benefits of the expectation effect and the self fulfilling prophecy (that we discussed in an earlier chapter).

3. End Goals & Means Goals

End goals are the ultimate outcomes or achievements we might aim for, such as starting a successful business, or reaching a certain level of financial independence or making an impact on the lives of others or even just living a happy and fulfilled life. They define our broader aspirations and the final destinations we want to reach. Means goals, on the other hand, are the steps or actions we can take to achieve those end goals. They are the specific objectives that we believe (or have been made to believe) will pave the way toward our larger ambitions or desires.

While means goals are an essential part of charting out our plan for reaching our end goals, it's easy to become overly focused on these intermediary steps and lose sight of the ultimate purpose. This phenomenon, known as *means-end inversion*, occurs when we become so engrossed in achieving our goals that we forget why we set them in the first place.

Let me tell you about one of my coaching clients who was building a tech startup in the domain of mental health. He had created means goals like securing venture capital funding, hiring top talent, onboarding therapists and expanding the customer base rapidly. Over time, he had become so fixated on these means goals—particularly the relentless pursuit of funding and rapid expansion—that he had lost sight of the original vision for the company.

This is not an isolated example, but a risk that all of us face with any end goal that we set for ourselves. And this is true not just for career or business, but even personal growth goals. For example, your end goal might be well-being, and you might get so fixated on the means goals of strictly following your workout, meditation, and journaling routines that they become burdensome, and overshadow your initial goal of achieving holistic well-being.

The antidote to avoid the means-end inversion trap, is to regularly reflect on and realign your chosen means goals with your end goal—ensuring that each step taken remains in service to your long term vision and purpose.

Another thing to remember is that when we create means goals, we are actually basing it on several assumptions. We might believe that doing one thing will lead to the other, but that might actually not be true. Also perhaps, there might be other ways to reach our desired end goal which we are not yet aware of.

So instead of looking at your means goal as a necessity, I would recommend that you start looking at it as a choice. This will allow your brain to see 'one possible path ahead', but also be willing to look out for other paths. More importantly, if you hit a roadblock or failure in your means goal, it will not devastate you. Nor will you give up or abandon your end goal. Your brain will instead start looking for other possibilities or routes around that particular block.

If thoughtfully created and used, goals can be one of the most transformative tools in your career crafting journey.

They have the power to unleash a more determined, focused, and driven version of yourself, helping you journey towards all the dreams you've ever had. Goals can serve as wonderful motivators that make you break out of stagnation and continuously grow into bolder and more upgraded versions of yourself.

I have found that setting goals has always helped me get better—irrespective of whether I have finally reached that particular goal or not! The key to unlocking all these auxiliary benefits of goal setting however is to follow approach B (described earlier through the mountain climbing example).

Effectuation versus Visioning

I started this chapter with the tenet that not everyone needs to set career goals and visions for themselves. And I am going to say that once again. You can do all the inner work that has been laid out in this book from chapters 1 to 9, and then use that as a foundation to craft your career forward, *without setting a larger predetermined vision.* This is an approach that some will prefer, and if you are one of them please go ahead - in fact there is a name for this method and its called *effectuation*. In this approach, you start with your current situation and incrementally keep leveraging what you already have in terms of your strengths, resources and network (basically the tree of life one pager that you made in chapter 9). At regular intervals you ask yourself, what next steps can I take to open up new possibilities?

Suppose you're thinking of changing jobs, you could just reach out to people you already know, such as former colleagues or acquaintances from professional events, for informational conversations. Just share your curiosity about new fields or roles with them, and listen to their insights with an open mind. Or you could volunteer for a project outside your immediate job responsibilities to just see where that might take you.

If you're not looking for a drastic change but want to feel more fulfilled in your current role, an effectuating approach will encourage you to experiment within your existing environment. You can identify areas within your current job where you can make a small but meaningful impact, such as proposing a new project, volunteering to lead a team initiative, or learning a new skill that could be valuable to your organization. By actively seeking out these opportunities, you can not only gain new experiences and expand your capabilities but also build a stronger reputation and network within your current workplace. This could lead to unexpected promotions, role expansions, or even the chance to pivot into a different area of the organization.

Each of these steps may seem small, but they are powerful because they're grounded in what you already have and know. They allow you to experiment and adapt without feeling overwhelmed by the need for a dream vision or perfect plan. In effectuation, it's not about knowing exactly where you're going, but about moving forward with curiosity and confidence, allowing the journey to reveal new and unexpected opportunities along the way.

As opposed to an effectuation approach, a career visioning approach starts with a clear, long-term vision of what you want to achieve and then creating specific goals and a strategic roadmap to reach that ideal future state. A visioning approach can be particularly powerful when you have a strong sense of your desired career destination, and it brings with it all the benefits of goal setting that we have discussed in this chapter—clarity, direction, motivation, purpose, and focus. By creating a compelling vision, we have literally created a personal north star that can guide our career decisions and actions, making it easier to recognize opportunities that align with our long-term goals. For example, if you envision becoming a leader in sustainable business practices, you can intentionally seek roles or projects that build relevant skills, knowledge, and networks in this area. A clear vision will also help you better communicate your career goals to others, attracting support, mentorship, partnerships, and even possible financing.

We have already done all the groundwork that you will need to to create a career vision in chapters 1 to 9. So if you would like to go the visioning route, sit down on a weekend and pull out all your notes - your values, success dimensions, ROTI list, and of course your tree of life. Think about the impact you want to make in the world, what energizes you and what kind of work makes you feel most alive. Pull out your notes from your future self visualization exercise where you imagined yourself five or ten years from now. Use inputs from all these reflections and start to shape them into a coherent picture of your desired career future. DRAW it out! I strongly believe that a picture is truly worth a thousand words when it comes to creating visions for our brain to work upon.

Both effectuation and visioning have their unique benefits, and you might find yourself more drawn to one than the other during different phases of your life. At times, especially early on when you might feel unsure about your ultimate goals, effectuation can help you explore diverse paths without the pressure of defining a long-term vision. As you gain experience and confidence, you might shift to a visioning approach, using what you've learned to set more specific goals and pursue a clearer path.

I've personally used both approaches at different times in my career. For instance, when I was just starting out as a freelancer (post a long salaried stint at IIM Bangalore), I leaned heavily on effectuation—I experimented with projects, and offerings, using my existing resources and networks - building on the opportunities that organically came my way. As I gained experience and began to better understand my coaching strengths and had built a personal brand in the domain, I created a vision for myself. Then again, within that larger vision, I have cycled back to effectuation, particularly when designing specific new offerings (like residential retreats). Embracing both methods has allowed me to be flexible, innovative, and open to opportunities, while also generally heading in a purposeful direction for myself.

Prototyping and Experimenting

No matter how much we reflect, discover, and vision, there's always something more to learn by actually *doing*—by test-driving (or prototyping) different parts of our future plans. It's like trying on clothes before you buy them. How do you know if that dress fits until you actually zip it up and twirl around in front of the mirror?

Prototyping in your career ideas works the same way, and you can include it in whatever approach you choose, effectuation or visioning.

Here's the thing: as deep and insightful as our inner work in the previous chapters might have been, our brains still do have their limits. Our inner work is always going to be work in progress and so there will still be more biases and patterns in our own sensemaking, keeping us locked in paradigms, and assumptions not yet uncovered. But when we step outside of our own minds, interact with others, and throw ourselves into uncharted territories, we unlock a whole new world of questions, insights, and aha moments that we'd never have stumbled upon just by reflecting in our heads

Take one of my clients, for example. She had this long-standing dream of owning her own organic farm. She'd been saving up for years, imagining the peaceful life she'd lead, surrounded by nature. But before diving headfirst into such a big commitment, I suggested she spend some time volunteering at a farm—just to get a real taste of what it involved. Two weeks in, she realized farm life wasn't she'd imagined it to be. That experience freed her from her previous fantasy and opened her up to explore other ways of making her life and work more fulfilling.

Prototyping isn't just about bursting bubbles, though. Sometimes, you'll find that you absolutely love the experiment you're trying out, and it will give you the confidence to go all-in on your dream. Or you might tweak and refine your ideas, making them even better suited to your life. Whatever the outcome, prototyping gives you valuable, low-cost feedback before you make any major life or career shifts.

Prototyping is a playful and insightful way to actually get your hands dirty and figure out what truly lights you up and what might just have been a borrowed fantasy. Afterall, like we saw in chapter 2 earlier, our brains have been filled up with so much programming from outside that even what can sometimes feel like a 'heartfelt desire' might just be another layer of programming in our brains waiting to be unmasked!

Dream on and Savour your Journey

Whether you choose an effectuation approach, a visioning approach, or a combination of both, don't forget to anchor yourself in a Hero Mindset. Also, adopt an experimental attitude and be flexible with the visions and goals you set as you craft your way forward. Your primary responsibility is to *show up each day* in support of your vision—or, if you're following the effectuation approach, in support of yourself—and give it your best effort. Celebrate every milestone along the way. Focus on the gains you've made—the progress across your own dimensions of success—rather than just the gap that remains between you and your ultimate goal or vision. After all, you're here for an exhilarating career crafting JOURNEY, aren't you

11

Portfolio Careers for Multipotentialites

"Don't try to fit me in a box… My life is not one dimensional. I'm the summer breeze and the hurricane… I'm the serene lake and the raging ocean… I'm the gentle poet and the rough warrior"

Steve Maraboli

We've all heard the well-meaning advice: "You just need to find that one perfect niche for yourself!" or "Once you discover the right field, your career will take off!"

It's an enticing promise, isn't it? The idea that somewhere out there is a singular, magical path that will transform your professional life into a dream come true. So, we embark on a quest, searching for 'The One'—that elusive job, passion, or calling that will make everything fall into place.

But is this notion universally applicable? Will it work for everyone? The popular image that springs to mind is often a Venn diagram, a neat little chart showing where your passions, talents, and what the world needs intersect. It's a pretty picture, and I have met several people who have been clinging to this ideal, hoping to someday discover their *'Ikigai'*. In fact, I have even had coaching clients come to me with a singular ask—to help them find their ikigai!

The Myth of One True Calling

The figure you're looking at is a 'supposed' pictorial representation of Ikigai,—which you will find floating all over the internet.

However, it's important to clarify that unlike what has been popularized, Ikigai is not just a Japanese version of 'self-help' aimed at discovering the single purpose of your life. The word itself is a combination of two Japanese terms: "iki," meaning 'living,' and "gai," meaning 'value' or 'worth.' In Japanese culture, Ikigai can indeed refer to life purpose, but it's not limited to that; it can also be something as simple as a daily ritual, like drinking tea.

However, let's return to the popularized version of Ikigai, depicted in the Venn diagram (or its variations) that most people associate with career discussions today. I believe it's essential to debunk ideas like this because, although they might be intended to inspire, they can sometimes lead to stress and unrealistic expectations. This notion reinforces the myth that everyone has 'one true calling' or a specific Ikigai.

While it's true that some people may discover one thing that they feel destined to do, and then lead a fulfilling life, this is not the case for everyone. Not everyone needs to have a single 'Ikigai' or life purpose, and believing you must find that one thing can leave you feeling dissatisfied or anxious.

Remember the story of the mountain climber who focused solely on the destination rather than the journey? Pursuing Ikigai in its popularized form can make you like that climber—so fixated on finding your supposed 'true calling' that you miss out on appreciating and investing in the journey itself.

There's also a subtle trap in the idea of 'finding your Ikigai,' and it lies in the verb that is being used for this process. The word 'finding' implies that something already exists out there for you to discover. But haven't we discussed how fulfilling careers are crafted and consciously created, rather than simply found? When we believe there's something out there waiting to be found, not finding it can feel like an ongoing personal failure, leading to chronic dissatisfaction and thoughts of *not good enough* or *not yet there*. Two very unhelpful categories of mental chatter indeed!

Let me clarify that not everyone will fall into these traps associated with the concept of Ikigai. It can indeed help or work in an inspiring way for some people. However, if you haven't yet found 'your one' how about exploring the alternate idea—a possibility of multiple callings!

Are You a 'Multipotentialite'

Multipotentialite is a term coined by career coach and community leader, Emilie Wapnick, to describe people who have many creative pursuits. The ones who can excel in many fields. The ones with many diverse interests.

Basically, the ones for whom the notion of 'one true calling' might not exist.

There is a spectrum under which Multipotentialites typically operate. On one end are Sequential multipotentialites—people who focus on one project at a time, wrapping it up before moving on to the next. On the other end are Simultaneous multipotentialites - people who thrive on juggling multiple projects at once. Most multipotentialites find themselves somewhere in between, and their approach need not be fixed—it can evolve over time. They might start out focusing on one thing at a time but shift to juggling several as they navigate different stages of life.

There are a lot of strengths that multipotentialites typically bring, and if by now you are starting to identify as being a multipotentialite yourself, read on below, this is for you.

You are likely to have the unique knowledge and opportunity to combine two or more concepts and create something new where they intersect; thereby being a leader in a new and unexplored field. What will also make you an asset in any professional setting is how easily and quickly you can learn new things and can adapt to different roles or contexts. As the bridge between different worlds, you have the potential and opportunity to connect people from different paradigms.

However there is a potential downside too! As a multipotentialite myself, I know that our constant craving for variety can be a double-edged sword, especially if it's not managed carefully.

Need for Variety

One of the main challenges that we multipotentialites face is fitting into the more conventional world of work. Our constant and high need for variety often makes it difficult for us to adjust and mould ourselves permanently for a single task, role, or project.

Even if we find something that we like, we cannot remain content with doing the same thing everyday for the rest of our lives. Or at least, not without changing how we do it. It is like we are wired with an inherent need to regularly switch what we are doing— whether that means shifting between different jobs or tackling multiple projects within the same role, either sequentially or simultaneously.

When our need for variety is not respected and fed, and we do not have that kind of flexibility in our lives, we get bored and frustrated at not being able to express ourselves and live up to our full potential.

You might be thinking, *"Isn't it a simple fix then to just keep doing many different things?"* Unfortunately, it's not as simple. The solution is a lot like walking on a tightrope.

With too little variety, we feel like we're being held back. But if we have too much of it, then we risk feeling burdened, overworked, and also the frustration of not being able to do everything as well as we would have liked to, simply because we do not have enough time to dedicate to everything.

This is in some ways similar to what we discussed regarding flow. To trigger the state of being in the zone, the flow state of peak performance, you need just the right level of challenge with respect to your skills. If the challenge doesn't push you to tap into your full potential, you'll likely feel bored, and achieving a state of flow will be hard to reach. However, if you attempt something that is far too difficult for your current skill level, you'll likely feel overwhelmed with anxiety, making it difficult again to achieve flow.

Similarly, the key for multipotentialites like us is to find the right level of variety, by observing ourselves. The 'right' level varies from one person to another. In fact, it can also vary for a single person during the different stages of his or her life.

So, where can this key be found? And how can it be correctly used to ensure that we don't end up toppling off from this tightrope that we need to walk upon?

The simple answer is trying out things to see what works. And that brings us to the immense importance of being experimental. Think of it like your career journey is unfolding in a big laboratory. Like a scientist, you need to closely monitor the observations, tweak around with your methods, and conduct experiments in real time to zero in on the level of variety you currently need. Ask yourself realtime questions like, *'Am I satisfied with my work right now?'*, *'Am I bored because of the lack of variety?*, *Am I overwhelmed because there is too much variety?*—and then make the adjustments or changes that you need to!

Finding ways to introduce variety and balance within a single line of work can often make your career more fulfilling. But if you crave a bit more adventure, consider a more strategic approach: juggling multiple jobs or roles simultaneously to satisfy your diverse interests—A Portfolio Career!

Crafting Portfolio Careers

Having a portfolio career is a bit like being a juggler, but instead of balls, you're managing roles, jobs and maybe even a prototyping project (that might have potential to turn into a job later)—all at once! It could mean freelancing while consulting, launching a startup while teaching part-time, and/or mixing in some prototyping projects as well. That's what my career looks like right now, and I crafted it to fit my life. But, hey, this path isn't for everyone, because it carries both risks and challenges.

I'm going to guide you through some steps below to help you figure out if a portfolio career approach might be a good fit for you. We'll revisit some of the inner work we've already done in previous chapters, but this time, to help us answer a focussed question of whether a portfolio career is your best bet.

<u>Step 1: Estimating your Financial Needs</u>

First things first—what does an abundant and rich life mean to you? And no, I don't mean what others think it should be. This is about *you*. Take some time to think through this question and list out the various things that come to your mind. Richness for some can include luxuries, homes, cars or sending their kids abroad for education. Richness for some others can mean more time with family and friends, or more travel, or living in nature. Once you have your list ready, ask yourself: can the money you currently have support this vision both now and in the future?

If the answer is yes, congrats—you're like a bird soaring in a sky of endless possibilities! You can pursue whatever makes you happy, regardless of the paycheck. Maybe you'll even realize you don't need a traditional career at all, and instead, fill your days with hobbies and pro bono projects that light you up.

If the answer is no, don't worry, you're not alone— rather you are like most people I know or have worked with (including myself). You need to spend some time pinpointing exactly how much money you'd need to feel that sense of abundance. This sub-step is really important because if you do not put down a figure, then there is a huge trap of feeling 'poor' no matter what you earn. I have worked with clients, across different income levels, who were trapped in the mindset of 'I can't modify my career because I need the money'— but when I asked them how much money they would like, they haven't ever done the math!

Once you do this math and arrive at a number, you'll be in a much better position to understand how much you can experiment with your career and how much financial risk you can afford to take.

<u>Step 2: ROTI—Return on Time Invested</u>

Remember the ROTI exercise you did in chapter 4? Now, it's time to bring out those notes again. If you can find a job (or already have one) that checks off most of this list *and* roughly meet your financial needs from Step 1, maybe a portfolio career isn't necessary for you. In that case, I'd say dive deep into this one job and keep progressively sculpting it to create more variety and learning for yourself within it.

But if your ROTI list can't be satisfied by a single role (and you feel unfulfilled because of that), then it's time to start exploring the possibilities of a portfolio career.

<u>Step 3: Exploring and Balancing Your Portfolio</u>

Now comes the fun part—brainstorming different jobs, projects, or roles you could take on. For this step I recommend going back to your Tree of Life exercise that you did in chapter 8. Let your eyes gaze over your strengths, treasure chest of possibilities, and network. You can also show the page where you have listed these to a friend or your Pod members and ask them to brainstorm with you. Make a list of different possible jobs you could do, or projects that you can undertake based on things that feel interesting to you, and where you can leverage at least some of your existing strengths. Once you make this list, Jot down the potential income from each. If you are clueless about the typical income in a certain job or role, pause the exercise and go do some research. Speak with people who might already be doing something in that field.

Next pull out your total desired income (the number you calculated in Step 1), and play with a few different combinations of the projects or gigs that you have listed to see how they total up in terms of expected income. Don't stress about being exact—this is just a rough estimate.

Pick each combination and next check how the different gigs within it match up with your ROTI@work list. Some projects might naturally fulfil certain items more than others. Ideally you would want to diversify them to meet your differing ROTI needs as well as your innate need for variety. Play around and iterate with different combinations until you create a starting point of a portfolio that somewhat meets your financial needs as well as your personal fulfilment (ROTI list).

Crafting your first portfolio combination of possible jobs or gigs is just the beginning. Once you embark on it, you'll need to review and tweak it periodically based on your experiences as well as external life situations (just like you review and manage your financial portfolio).

Besides the safety aspect of having many income channels to rely upon, a portfolio career also works wonders in letting you preserve and exercise your autonomy. I have personally experienced this. Once I moved to a portfolio career, I became be a bolder version of myself - only choosing to do the things that really resonated with me (without being under any pressure of being a 'yes-man'). Since my entire earnings were not tied down to one stream, I could also take more risks, be more creative, and try radical ideas.

In recent years, I've tried out various online group programs and digital products, experimenting with risky business models that were far from guaranteed in terms of profitability. What made this possible? I had steady, reliable projects in my portfolio, like my teaching at IIM Bangalore and corporate workshops, and these were my safety net.

Do remember that no single job in your portfolio needs to satisfy all your ROTI@work items. One might fulfill your need for creativity, while another helps you leave a legacy. With a portfolio career, you get to mix and match, crafting a professional life that's as dynamic and multifaceted as you are.

Avoiding Pitfalls of a Portfolio Career

Embarking on a portfolio career is an exciting choice that can open up a world of opportunities. But like any adventure, it comes with its own set of challenges. If not managed thoughtfully, it can lead to burnout and make you question your decision. Here are some tips - *all learnt the hard way!*

1. While diversifying, and especially before saying *'Yes'* to yet one more thing, pause and check existing project timelines - be sure not to overcommit. Take a fair assessment of your capabilities, time, and other factors and only take on things to an extent that is realistically possible to achieve.

2. The demands of a portfolio career can become all-consuming, and could lead to self-neglect—health or otherwise. So prioritize yourself and your time too, set boundaries, build in *regular self care rituals*, and maintain a time buffer for unpredictable work surges or personal crises.

3. *Do not compare* your progress with anyone else. Remember as you are a unique person, your portfolio will be an even more unique portfolio and therefore any comparison is going to be irrational, unfair and will either lead to a false sense of superiority or to heartbreak. And definitely don't compare your progress in what you undertake as a part-time gig with the achievements of someone else who is doing it full time!

Embracing a portfolio career is not just a career choice—it's an ongoing process of learning, adapting, and self-discovery. It is a journey that requires you to regularly evaluate your path, adjust your strategies, and strike a balance between your short term and long term goals. Think of it like managing a financial portfolio: just as successful investors keep their long-term vision in mind, your career portfolio will thrive when you maintain a clear sense of direction and remain committed to growth and learning.

Ultimately, each individual project, whether it succeeds or fails, is an investment in your future. Every experience can contribute to your development, helping you become more robust and versatile as long as you retain the right approach—a Hero and Growth mindset. It takes courage and creativity to embark on a portfolio career, but the rewards are truly worth it. You get to live a rich and multifaceted life—one that is truly deserving of the versatile multipotentialite that you are!

12

Managing Conflicts Along Your Journey

"Every conflict we face in life is rich with positive and negative potential. It can be a source of inspiration, enlightenment, learning, transformation, and growth—or rage, fear, shame, entrapment, and resistance."

Kenneth Cloke

When I was a child, I was taught to avoid challenging or disagreeing with my parents or teachers. Many of you might relate to that, right? The message was clear: being agreeable and keeping the peace was rewarded, while confrontation was seen as something negative, to be avoided. This shaped how many of us saw conflict—something to dodge at all costs.

But can we really live our lives, especially in our work, without encountering conflict? The truth is, we can't.

My perspective on conflict began to shift during my PhD at London Business School. As I studied the different types of conflict, I discovered something crucial—not all conflict is bad. In fact, when there's no conflict at all, it can actually mean stagnation. If no one is questioning the status quo, it could be that creativity is being stifled, that growth is being held back. This was a game-changer for me. Suddenly, conflict wasn't something to be feared but something that could spark progress.

Think about it: without conflict, how do we challenge the old ways of thinking? Where would innovation come from? When managed thoughtfully, conflict can be the spark that ignites creativity. It encourages collaboration, problem-solving, and new perspectives—things that might have otherwise gone unnoticed.

In your career, conflicts are bound to show up. But instead of seeing them as roadblocks or failures, I invite you to reframe them. Just like failure often leads to success, conflict can lead to creativity, innovation, and growth. It's an opportunity to strengthen relationships, refine ideas, and challenge outdated patterns that might no longer serve you or your organization.

This chapter isn't about trying to eliminate conflict from your life—that's neither possible nor desirable. Instead, it's about learning how to handle conflict when it comes up. With the right mindset and tools, conflict can become a powerful driver of positive change—both in your personal growth and in the places where you work.

You will learn how to turn what may initially seem like an obstacle into a powerful catalyst for your career growth.

Types of Conflicts

Not all conflicts are created equal. They can crop up in different situations for different reasons, and they tend to trigger us in very unique ways. That's why it's important to recognize that not every conflict can (or should) be handled the same way.

Task Conflicts: These conflicts arise when individuals disagree about what needs to be done or about the goals they're working toward. Think of it as a tug-of-war over ideas or priorities—each person has a different vision of what the outcome should be. Task conflicts can also show up as clashes in viewpoints or different interpretations of a problem. But here's the thing: when managed right, task conflicts can be super productive! They can fuel creativity and help teams come up with better solutions.

Relationship Conflicts: Also known as Emotional or Interpersonal Conflicts, these happen when there's friction between individuals, often due to personality clashes. It's the classic "I just don't like them" situation. Relationship conflicts can be the most draining because they're personal. When these arise, it's usually less about the work and more about the underlying emotions—grudges, misinterpretations, or a simple lack of trust.

Process Conflicts: At first glance, these might look like a subset of task conflicts, but they deserve their own spotlight. While task conflicts are about what needs to be done, process conflicts revolve around how it's done. You might agree with a colleague on the end goal, but you may not agree on the best steps to get there. Disagreements about timelines, methodologies, or roles fall under process conflicts. This type of conflict can either slow down progress or push teams to find more efficient ways to work together, depending on how it's handled.

Value Conflicts: Values are at the core of who we are—our guiding principles. They shape our decisions, our behaviors, and even our priorities. So when someone else's values don't align with ours, a value conflict emerges. These conflicts can feel particularly intense because they strike at the heart of what we stand for. Imagine working in an organization where profit is the top priority, but you deeply value sustainability. That's where the tug-of-war begins, and resolving this type of conflict often requires finding common ground or shared values.

We're not here to put each type of conflict into rigid categories of "good" or "bad"—that will depend on how you navigate through it. Think of the next section as your playbook. I'll introduce you to research-backed insights and a basic understanding of the typical effects of these different types of conflicts. But ultimately, the real test comes in how you apply these strategies to your unique circumstances. Remember, conflicts don't have to be a roadblock—they can be a signal that you're growing, evolving, and pushing boundaries. You always have the power to turn any conflict into a moment of learning or progress, or an opportunity to better understand and connect with the other people that you work with. And that is the primary objective of everything that I am going to share in the remaining sections of this chapter.

Balancing Productive and Destructive Forces

First lets look at task conflicts. These can be a delightful ally, proving useful nearly 90% of the time they come our way! They spark creativity, inspire fresh ideas, and open the door to vibrant brainstorming sessions. Think of them as the fuel for growth, innovation, and a sense of aliveness. And the best part? It's not just a hunch; it's backed by solid research!

So, the next time you find yourself facing a task conflict, pause for a moment. Ask yourself: How can I turn this into an opportunity to explore something exciting and new? Your answer could shape your unique experience and help you embrace these conflicts as an exciting and contributive part of your journey.

Unfortunately I don't have such good news for you with regard to relationship conflicts. These mostly stem from personal dislike and aren't quite as helpful. In fact research suggests they tend to be unproductive about 80-90% of the time. When these conflicts arise, it's easy to get caught up in tension and stress, which can distract us from what truly matters. You might find yourself opposing ideas simply because you don't see eye to eye with the person presenting them, or vice versa.

While there might be rare moments of growth from these conflicts, statistically, they're not the kind of experiences we want to gather too many of. Instead, I would recommend navigating around them whenever possible. If the person you are working with is a repeated collaborator or co-founder, then you can also seek relationship therapy or counselling.

Next, let's explore Process Conflicts—the mixed bag of conflict types! These can lead us to discover better, faster, and smarter ways to tackle tasks. However, there's a delicate balance to strike: while they can be insightful, they can also bring things to a standstill. Imagine sitting on a treasure trove of ideas, with everyone aligned on what needs to be done. Yet, if there's no agreement on how to do it, we might find ourselves stuck.

The key here is to assess each instance of process conflict individually. Tune in to whether it's guiding you toward innovation or holding you back in inaction. This awareness can empower you to either embrace these conflicts or approach them with caution.

And then we have value conflicts—they're like the hard teachers on our journey! Understanding their complexity has truly expanded my perspective and helped me receive the hidden gifts that such conflicts might bring.

For a long time, I viewed every situation through my own lens, and when something clashed with my values, I used to feel baffled or even frustrated. But once I began to recognize that everyone has their own set of deeply held values it became a game-changer! Just this understanding can open up a whole new realm of win-win possibilities in our collaborations with the other party or person.

When we accept that our truth isn't the only truth and that our perspective isn't the sole valid viewpoint, we can find creative ways to manage value conflicts without letting our ego get in the way. We will also have better clarity on when it might actually be best to simply walk away because their might exist no common ground at all for happy collaboration.

On the flip side, being rigid and convinced that our values are the only ones that matter can lead to very nasty situations. We might feel like literally shaking another person and insist, "This is the right way! Why can't you see it?!" History is littered with conflicts where one side sought to impose its values on another, often leading to significant strife and suffering. This serves as a powerful reminder of the importance of empathy and understanding in our interactions.

As you navigate your career crafting journey, consider approaching Value Conflicts with a mindset of curiosity and collaboration. Instead of trying to convert others to your perspective, seek to understand their viewpoints. This openness can transform potential conflicts into rich opportunities for connection and innovation, enriching both your professional life and the lives of those around you.

Three Slippery Slopes to Watch Out For

In the theoretical knowledge we've set out to gain, it's relatively easy to differentiate between various types of conflict. However, in practice, navigating these conflicts can be quite challenging. There are multiple slippery slopes, and you need to be aware of them.

For example, when your emotions run high, you might find it difficult to remember that disagreements are often just differences in opinion. You may not be thinking, "This is just a disagreement about our approach; I shouldn't take this personally." Instead, your mental chatter might be saying, "Why is this person attacking me? They must not like my ideas!"

This way one type of conflict can easily give rise to another. When that happens, conflicts can escalate, becoming much more problematic and challenging. Each conflict type we discussed can trigger the others and the speed at which one type of conflict can transform into another is often overlooked.

Let's explore three specific cases that are particularly tricky when collaborating with other people on our career journeys. By being equipped to spot these slippery slopes, you can prevent unconscious and rapid escalation.

Task Conflicts Turning into Relationship Conflicts: Imagine a team with two distinct personalities, Person A thrives on creativity and innovation, while Person B values structure and logic. Person A suggests a vibrant, color-coded report for an upcoming presentation, focusing on storytelling through visuals. In contrast, Person B insists on a more traditional, data-driven PowerPoint presentation filled with charts and numbers. Person A's proposal is met with scepticism and resistance from Person B.

Initially, this disagreement is about the task at hand—how to present information. However, as discussions continue, Person A may begin to feel personally rejected. Their brain might interpret Person B's counterarguments as a sign of personal disapproval, leading to feelings of inadequacy.

So how can we prevent such instances of task conflict from turning into relationship conflict? If you find yourself in a similar position as Person A, first acknowledge the situation. Remind yourself that the disagreement is about the idea, not your worth as an individual. Instead of thinking, "Person B doesn't like my idea because they don't like me," focus on the disagreement itself. Communicate clearly: "I see we have different approaches to this report. Can we explore how both ideas might work together?"

For Person B, it's essential to avoid personalizing the disagreement. Acknowledge that Person A's creativity doesn't diminish the value of data. Clarify your stance: "I appreciate your perspective, but I believe our audience will respond better to a structured approach." This way, the focus remains on the task rather than personal feelings.

Process Conflicts Turning into Relationship Conflicts: Process conflicts arise when team members disagree on how to execute an agreed-upon task. Consider a scenario where a project team has agreed to develop a marketing strategy for a new product. Person A proposes a rapid deployment strategy to get the product to market quickly, while Person B suggests a more measured approach involving extensive market research before launch.

Initially, this is a process conflict about the execution of a shared goal. However, if tensions rise, Person A might feel that

Person B is undermining their expertise or speed, perceiving it as a personal challenge to their capabilities.

To mitigate these kinds of slippery slopes, both parties should remember to keep bringing back their focus to the common goal: launching a successful product. Even if the other person forgets, you can regularly remind him or her of your shared objective. For example, Person A could say, "I understand we have different approaches, but our goal is to launch successfully. How can we combine our strategies to achieve that?" This keeps the conversation constructive and focused on the common objective or agreed upon task.

Value Conflicts Turning into Task or Process Conflicts: In my youth I used to experience this type of conflict again and again in my life. And for most of the time, I wasn't even aware that this was what was happening. But now that I can identify these, I find myself equipped to handle them much better.

Let me give you an example. During my MBA days, class debates often became intense. I recall one memorable instance when a fellow student came to assault me physically because the points I was making were completely at odds with his value system, and I was not giving up. Without realizing it, I was treating the debate as a purely academic exercise, focused on proving my point, rather than recognizing that we were actually clashing over our core values. On the face of it, we were in a Task Conflict—but it had actually been triggered by a Value Conflict.

Sometimes, differing values can also lead to disagreements about processes, particularly if team members are not aware of the underlying issues at play. Imagine a team working on a community project where one member prioritizes efficiency while another emphasizes inclusivity. This could lead to a process conflict when the efficiency-oriented member pushes for quick decisions, while the inclusivity-minded member advocates for extensive community consultations before proceeding.

Whenever you find yourself in a situation where differing values are at play, it's crucial to navigate the conversation with awareness and empathy. Acknowledge that both parties may hold strong beliefs, and rather than getting entrenched in a debate, aim to understand the underlying motivations behind each other's perspectives. This can transform the interaction from a combative stance into a more collaborative exploration of ideas. By opening up a dialogue that respects differing values, you create space for innovative solutions that integrate diverse viewpoints.

With process related disagreements, it's vital to acknowledge the differences in values while still striving for a common goal. Remind the team of the project's objectives. For instance, the efficiency-oriented member might say, "I know we value inclusivity, but how can we balance that with the need for timely decisions?" This dialogue can help maintain respect for different values while focusing on achieving the project's goals together.

In later years of my career, I have often found some very wonderful innovations come out of task or process conflicts that were rooted in a value conflict. However, this can happen only when the conflict is managed empathetically and sensitively. By being mindful of these slippery slopes, you can foster a more harmonious work environment.

Every interaction presents an opportunity to build connections and cultivate understanding. So why not embrace these moments as chances for growth, and let your awareness guide you towards creating more value as well as understanding—for both yourself, as well as the other person(s) involved.

Internal Stances from a BEING Standpoint

Let's take a moment to reflect on the Tree of Life exercise. Remember how we separated the 'being' aspects from the 'doing' aspects of our lives? The doing encompasses all those actions and behaviours that fill our days. But here's the key: we are human BEINGS, not merely human DOINGS! The internal stance we choose to adopt is the essence of who we are, and from this foundation of being, our actions will naturally flow. Over the years, I've discovered certain powerful stances of 'Being' that can help us manage and navigate external conflicts with more grace and ease.

Non-judgment: This stance is about stepping back from labels like 'right' or 'wrong,' and 'good' or 'bad.' You already know that our bounded awareness often prevents us from seeing the whole picture, so why jump to conclusions. Think about how many conflicts arise because each party believes they hold the ultimate truth. By simply recognizing that our perspectives differ, we can often stop conflicts before they escalate. When we let go of the need to insist that our beliefs are the 'right' one, we create more space for healthy discussions and understanding.

Empathy: This stance invites us to step into someone else's shoes, truly seeing and feeling where they're coming from. Imagine engaging in a dialogue where each person actively listens and seeks to understand. When empathy takes centre stage, it fosters an atmosphere of respect and kindness. The beautiful part? With everyone adopting this mindset, the need for conflicts diminishes significantly. It's as if we are creating a safety net that catches misunderstandings before they fall into deeper disagreements.

Curiosity: Think about how children handle conflicts. One minute they're arguing, and the next, they're back to laughing and playing together. That sense of curiosity (which we often lose as adults) can be a powerful tool in conflict resolution. When faced with differing opinions, we can ask ourselves, "I wonder why she suggested that? What could happen if we tried it that way?" Such genuine curiosity opens us up to new ideas and experiences, transforming potential conflicts into opportunities for learning and growth.

Playfulness: This one is actually a potent but highly underrated stance. Let's revisit the story of Person A and Person B that we discussed as an example earlier. Imagine if, instead of allowing disagreements to spiral, they approached their differences with a sense of humour. What if they laughed together, acknowledging, "Wow, we really see the world differently!" This light-heartedness can turn a potential clash into a shared moment of connection, preventing the escalation of egos and emotions that often lead to deeper conflicts. It's a delightful reminder that sometimes, laughter truly is the best medicine!

Willingness to Let Go: So often, we enter discussions with a fixed mindset, convinced that our perspective is the only valid one or correct one. This rigidity can fuel conflict. But what if we allowed ourselves to be open to new ideas? Embracing the notion of letting go doesn't mean we're losing; it means we're gaining the strength to consider that other viewpoints might also hold value. It means we are willing to upgrade and revise our ideas and points of view. It means we are mature enough to let go of an idea that we might have been attached to, because now we have discovered better ideas. Imagine the richness of collaboration that can emerge when we approach discussions and collaborations with this kind of an attitude.

Holding an Opposable Mind: This is yet another fascinating mental stance that has been popularized by management expert, Roger Martin. It invites us to acknowledge that our personal truth is just that—personal. Our experiences shape our beliefs, but they don't define the ultimate truth. By cultivating an opposable mind, we become open to recognizing that there are many truths out there, each with its own validity. We are willing for others to challenge our beliefs and assumptions—to oppose our ideas. This openness enriches our interactions and helps us embrace diversity in values, perspectives, thoughts, and objectives.

Transforming Conflicts into Collaboration

In a world where we often find ourselves working alongside collaborators, teams, clients, and business partners, the art of navigating relationships becomes not just a skill but a vital necessity. By being more mindful of the different kinds of conflicts and their differing attributes, we can become better at creating spaces that foster connection, understanding, and mutual growth. We can learn to be more proactive, rather than reactive, and look for ways to transform potential conflicts into opportunities for collaboration and innovation.

As we navigate our careers and the intricate web of relationships that come with them, it's essential to remember that our external (visible) behaviour is seeded through the internal (invisible) stances that we take. Embracing non-judgment, empathy, curiosity, playfulness, a willingness to let go, an opposable mind, and a readiness to be wrong equips us with powerful behaviours for conflict management and collaboration. These stances lead to the creation of environments where open communication thrives, and diverse perspectives are not only welcomed but celebrated.

I do want to mention here, however, that not every conflict you encounter can be transformed into a journey of collaboration. Sometimes, despite all your efforts, it just might not happen—and perhaps it's not even possible. In these moments, the theories and stances shared in this chapter can still help you cultivate internal peace, even if external peace remains out of reach.

I learned this through my own involvement in a heartbreaking conflict that stretched on for more than two years, involving street dogs on the campus where I lived. It was essentially a gang war: two dogs who had lived on our street for years were being attacked daily by a new group of four dogs who would invade their territory. These battles could be brutal, and whenever I was on the street, I would fiercely defend "my" street dogs. I had formed a deep bond with them, and they were the ones under attack. When I stood on their side, the invading dogs would growl and lunge at me, seeing me as their enemy.

But one morning, while I was meditating in the stadium (away from my street), something extraordinary happened. One of the "invader" dogs came and sat peacefully beside me, joining me in the quiet bliss of the moment. I didn't even notice her until I opened my eyes. She gave me a gentle, loving gaze, inviting me to pet her.

It was a surreal but powerful wake-up call for me. Even this dog knew how to separate task conflict from relationship conflict. She understood that when she was on my street, I posed a threat to her—but out here in the stadium, she simply wanted to share in the peace and calm.

This dog taught me one of my most profound learnings in conflict management. Later that day, when the gang returned to attack, I was back on the street, chasing them away with sticks and stones. But even as I hurled the stones, I felt nothing but love for the dogs I was trying to ward off.

As you move forward, remember that crafting your adventurous career isn't just about the destinations you reach but also the relationships you build, and the learnings that you learn along the way. Each interaction is a chance to practice the stances that we discussed in this chapter, to weave empathy into your interactions, and to approach situations with non-judgment, curiosity and playfulness. In doing so, you empower yourself and those around you to grow and thrive in an ever-evolving landscape.

My hope is that you embrace the outwardly messy and sometimes even ugly conflict situations in your career, with inner mindfulness and confidence. Remember that every conflict managed with grace can bring you closer to the career and life you envision—one full of richness, joy, purpose, and meaningful connections.

13

Co-creating with Energy Flows

"We are not human beings having a spiritual experience; we are
spiritual beings having a human experience."

Pierre Teilhard de Chardin.

This chapter might not be for everyone, and that's okay. If that
quote resonated with you, then you're likely in the right place. If it
didn't, or if you find yourself feeling sceptical or unsure, that's
completely valid too. I know this because I have people I care
about—family, friends, clients, and students—who sit on both sides
of this divide. I understand the resistance that can come with this
territory.

There was a time in my life when I put a lot of energy into
gathering 'scientific evidence' to try and convince the people close
to me about the existence of invisible forces and the benefits of
working with subtle energies. I thought that if I just found enough
proof, I could get them to see and believe what I had experienced.
But I eventually learned that trying to prove something beyond the
current frameworks of science only left me exhausted. More
importantly, as I deepened my connection with my spiritual guides,
I realized that it wasn't my job to prove anything. Instead, I was
meant to live by example, to be a role model by sharing my own
experiences—what worked, what didn't—and allowing others to

take what they want from my story, experiment on their own, and draw their own conclusions.

So, if this chapter feels too far out of your mental comfort zone, that's okay. There's no need to push yourself into something that doesn't feel right. You can still enjoy and benefit from everything else in this book. Just skip ahead to Chapter 14, and you won't miss a beat.

But if that quote sparked a little curiosity, if you're feeling the slightest pull to explore further, then make yourself a warm cup of tea, settle in, and let me share with you the adventures I've had in engaging with these invisible realms. This isn't about proving anything to anyone. It's about offering you the possibility to explore, to see where these energies might take you, and to trust that whatever you take away from this chapter will be just right for you.

Re-legitimizing a Natural Awareness through Structured Lessons

Most children naturally play with energy, even without realizing it. Their playground is made of both the seen and unseen woven together as a well-knit fabric, one in which imagination, awareness and observation are all closely intertwined—and seldom questioned. I was no different. As I grew older however, and gained more understanding and vocabulary, I began to notice that there were certain things in my own awareness and experience that words couldn't quite capture. These experiences couldn't be easily articulated and I found myself in a curious predicament: I could feel things, but I couldn't always express them, not even to myself. Art and poetry slowly became my bridge between those invisible realms and the material world, allowing me to share glimpses of the unspoken energies I experienced.

I explored these magical spaces through flower arrangements, dance, and other creative projects. These weren't just hobbies—they were deep, transcendent connections and I just don't have words to convey the full richness of what I experienced during these activities.

As I grew older, I began to live in two distinct worlds. In one, I was a dreamer, inhabiting an invisible world that was private, unshared. In the other, I was an intellectual, sharp and logical in school and other structured forums. Logic ruled one part of me, while intuition governed the other. For a long time, I kept these two worlds separate. I had a high need for acceptance and approval from the adults around me, and I found that maintaining this split helped me navigate my life without conflict.

Naturally drawn to forms of meditation, I intuitively explored practices like chanting, flame gazing, and communing with nature. These were my sacred escapes, a way of dissolving into a trance-like state that felt like home. However, I convinced myself these experiences were private, and separate from the 'real world.'

Then, when I was 12 years old, I had a near-death experience. I was part of a fire accident (and stampede) in the town of Jamshedpur, that claimed hundreds lives—including some of my own friends who were sitting right beside me at the event. I too was caught in the stampede, and at one point I sort of zoned out and entered a trance like state. There was a kind of peace and focussed awareness and all noise outside faded into the background and I heard just one voice that told me exactly what to do and how to get out. First, it told me to close my mouth and stay silent, I had been screaming and hollering before that. I literally heard the words, *"sound is a form of energy so don't waste it "*, and I was reminded of the chapter in my 6'th grade science textbook where we were learning about sound. Then the voice told me to look up, and I saw a tiny little patch of sky beyond the layers of burnt bodies and wooden pillars that I was buried under. The voice told me to look only at that patch of sky and keep climbing towards it, which I systematically did. Even after that I kept receiving specific guidance (like a mental dictation) on where to walk, and whom to ask for assistance and so on till I eventually found my way to a bed in the ICU of the local hospital where I was given anaesthesia.

Throughout the experience (till I lost consciousness), I was receiving remarkably specific guidance, as well as being surrounded by a surreal field of energetic presence and soothing. I was held in a field of energy both inside and outside of my own body which meant that I could feel the intensity of the first degree burns on my skin, but I wasn't inside the pain, I was feeling it from outside as if it was on another person and those sensations were being transmitted to me as information.

Even throughout my recovery period I felt engulfed in a peaceful bubble of universal love. My mother was really surprised at my cheerful demeanour despite having first degree burns and a head injury. I too struggled with the duality of the peace that I was experiencing internally and the painful emotions that were present all around in other people's worlds—for many known people had been killed or injured in the accident. I also experienced a conflict between my inner world (where death somehow didn't feel so intimidating), and the outer world where everyone was in deep mourning about the deaths that had occurred. I was a child, and I didn't want to appear strange, and so I kept my inner experience to myself and did not talk about it with anyone else.

At the age of seventeen, I attended my first Reiki course. By then, my cognitive thinking had become deeply entrenched in scientific and mathematical frameworks. But Reiki—this pure flow of Life Force Energy—was not bound by those hardened layers of intellect. It still found its pathways to flow, moving through my energy centres (chakras), that were yet untouched by my brains doubts and scepticism. In hindsight I realize, that my brain had given in to peer pressure (remember the Asch experiments on conformity) and along with a few friends who were also attending the class, I would analyze, critique, and poke fun at the teacher.

Yet, the Reiki flowed through my body–independent of my apprehensions and misgivings, independent of my judgements of the teacher, independent of my judgements of Reiki even–for Reiki was Reiki! Pure Life Force Energy in Motion. I'm forever grateful to my Reiki teacher for those first energetic attunements because (I have realized in hindsight) that they marked the moment when my two separate inner worlds (mental models) began to at least exchange information with each other.

In those early years, I confined Reiki to what I had been taught—using it solely as a body healing tool, and even then, only sparingly. Looking back, I am amazed at my own naivety. Why did I restrict something so profound to just addressing physical aches? Reiki could have been a tool for so much more, but my mind had created a model: Reiki is for healing, and healing means dealing with the physical body. And that's the only way I used it for quite many years.

After Reiki, I went on to explore many other mind-body-energy practices. Some are well-known, like Yoga, Vipassana, Mindfulness, and Chakra Meditation, while others are lesser-known modalities taught by different teachers and schools. I literally learnt every technique that came my way—Breathwork, Hypnosis, Astral Projection, Theta Healing, Access Consciousness, EFT, to name a few. Why so many courses you might ask? I was fighting an inner war all along—the part of me that could experience the non-physical was desperately trying to convince and prove to the other part of me that was sceptical and doubtful.

Meanwhile, my Angels and the universe made sure that I also continued to experience many more 'miracles' and 'other worldly experiences'. Some of these experiences spooked me out at times (because they seemed too weird to my rational brain) and I would go into a shell and not do any 'energy work' for months together.

But these were always temporary breaks only—something would always draw me back to metaphysical schools and courses. A chance encounter, a flyer found on a metro train, a book loaned by a friend, a video popped up by the internet algorithms. In hindsight I realize I was searching for a structured way to legitimize and understand better all the unstructured miracles and magic that I was naturally experiencing. And each of these courses and teachers have helped with parts of this long winding journey of understanding, assimilating, normalizing and eventually accepting —accepting that this too was 'normal' (in some circles at least) and that I was not alone or crazy.

However, even after attending all these programs and workshops, I do not claim to be an expert on energy practices. This field is way too vast, and I am still just a learner myself. So what I'll be sharing with you in this book are some basic energy tools—simple but powerful—designed to (a) complement the cognitive work you're doing in other chapters, and (b) be an invitation to explore more, should you wish to.

It's worth noting that every school of energy practice has its own rules about what can be taught to others, especially publicly. Many of the techniques can only be taught by certified teachers and in specific sequences (based on levels of classes and mastery). However, there are also general tools that can be shared more openly with anyone, and I've made sure to honor those guidelines in this chapter as I introduce you to simple but effective energy practices that you can experiment with.

Energy Tools for Managing Yourself and Your Career

As we get started with the exciting world of energy tools, I want to emphasize that what I'm sharing here is just a brief introduction to some simple tools and how I typically use them. To make it even easier for you, I have created video recordings of follow-along versions of some of them—specifically tailored for the context of career crafting—on the resources page of my website. Since these videos are designed for you to follow along, there's no need to have any prior training (or extra instructions apart from whatever is there in the video) to start benefitting from the practice.

That said, I must emphasize that to experiment more creatively with these tools and customize them for various contexts, it's better to learn the fundamentals of energy practices and techniques yourself, ideally in person, and from a certified teacher or institution.

So, consider the contents of this chapter as a basic starter menu that I have put together for you. I've used generic and easily understandable names for each tool, but remember that they may be known by different names within specific energy management schools or modalities.

Each of these ten tools or practices can be practiced with specific career visions or more generally with a broader attitude of surrendering to the Divine Will and purpose of the universe itself. Yes, you can absolutely embrace both of these approaches in your career crafting journey! It's not a matter of one versus the other, despite what some teachers and philosophies might suggest. I see it more as your own little career purpose forming a subset of the larger universal purpose.

So here's the starter menu, with a short explanation of each tool and some suggestions on career crafting contexts in which you can use them. You can also access the book resources page for recorded video guides, where you can do some of these as 'follow along exercises'.

Blessing Balls: You can think of these as visualized spheres filled with positive affirmations and energies aimed at attracting supportive circumstances. The technique involves creating a vibrant sphere in your mind (or as an invisible energetic ball that you hold between your hands), and filling it with light and positive intentions, which you can project towards specific projects or people or even just for yourself.

For instance, you might create a Blessing Ball filled with affirmations about your abilities and potential before an important job interview or presentation and then bathe yourself with that light or energy. You can also create blessing balls specifically to send to people you love, or even groups of people who might be going through challenging times. There are literally infinite ways in which you can charge and use a blessing ball for yourself or for others.

Energy Pull: This technique involves drawing in vibrant energy from the universe to replenish your own. The practice allows you to connect with universal energy, inviting it into your space to rejuvenate and uplift your personal energy centres, aura and surrounding field. By visualizing the energy entering your body, you can counteract feelings of fatigue or overwhelm, creating a balanced state of mind and body conducive to focused action.

You can also combine an energy pull with an energy ball that you create to symbolize a certain project or vision, and then draw in universal energies to charge up this energy ball and then send that energy out towards the vision of the particular project. You can also use energy pulls to energize spaces like your office or home or any auditorium or room where you plan to give a talk or hold a workshop. And you can do this in advance, it does not have to be done in real time.

Pillar of Light: This is one of my absolute favourites and its most common use is to create a protective space filled with strength and confidence. Imagine that your body encapsulated within a pillar of light whose top is anchored to the sun above (or a light source emanating from any Divine deity or God). Now visualize that the bottom of this pillar is connected to the centre of the planet earth and its live breathing Magma-like Mother earth energy. Allow the energies from above and below to flow freely up and down your pillar of light, cleansing and charging you as it does so.

When you visualize yourself within a Pillar of Light, you can cultivate feelings of safety and empowerment, allowing you to stand firm against external challenges. This practice can be particularly useful when facing difficult situations, or navigating uncertain paths.

EFT (Tapping): The EFT (Emotional Freedom Techniques) Tapping sequence involves tapping on specific points on the body while voicing thoughts and emotions to release blockages in your system. This tool combines aspects of psychology and acupressure, helping you to address emotional disturbances that may be hindering your wellbeing or progress. By focusing on specific issues while tapping, you can alleviate stress, cut through limiting beliefs in the mind, release embodied trauma and also foster a more positive mindset.

EFT is a really powerful tool and it can be used to relieve physical, mental, emotional, and energetic blockages. In fact once you experiment with EFT you will soon realize how interconnected all four of these are. There might be an emotional anxiety that is manifesting as a physical pain, and when you tap on the pain, the emotion arises, and then when you continue to tap on the emotion, a limiting belief that is creating that anxiety comes into your awareness and then when you tap on the belief and release it, suddenly your original physical pain might go away. I love EFT, because you can get started with any external symptom and as you tap, the symptoms that keep unfolding will themselves take you to the root cause.

EFT is a particularly useful tool to use whenever we hit any kind of upper limit in our own expansion or notice that we are self-sabotaging our own success or growth.

Consciousness Expansion: This is a simple but beautiful technique that opens your awareness to your true nature as an infinite and unbounded being. Sometimes when I guide my workshop participants through this exercise, I refer it as a pure awareness exercise. It is a practice where we acknowledge that while we are aware of the sensations of our body we are not actually the body itself. Then we acknowledge that while we can witness, and even consciously choose our thoughts, we are not the same as our thoughts. Then we further acknowledge that while we can feel the effect of our emotions, and even manage or manipulate our emotions, we are not the emotions themselves.

After progressing through these three stages, we are still left with an awareness, and this pure conscious awareness is what we are as a being. The consciousness of our being has no size or bonded space and so we allow it to expand beyond our body. Systematically, we allow it to continue expanding till we expand beyond planet earth, and further as far out into space as we want to go.

From this unbounded perspective of pure awareness we can look back at ourselves, our body, our thoughts, emotions, and any other situations in our life. The insights that we can get from this place is very different from what we get when we are strongly identified as our body, mind or emotions. This practice allows you to transcend your current perceptions and limitations, enabling a broader view of your life, career, specific situations and you're your own potential. This is a really versatile practice and you can customize it to use it to get through challenging times, destress yourself, find creative breakthroughs on a project, find ways to resolve conflicts and so many other things.

Cutting Cords: Energetic cord cutting is a powerful practice that helps you release past or current ties that no longer serve your growth. These ties, or "cords," represent lingering emotional attachments to people, places, jobs, or even past versions of yourself. By visualizing these cords and intentionally cutting them, you free yourself from emotional weight, creating space for healthier, more fulfilling connections and experiences.

At its core, cord cutting is about recognizing the relationships or situations that continue to drain your energy, (sometimes even after they've ended or served their purpose). This could be a past relationship that still affects you emotionally, a job that you left but continue to carry emotional baggage from, or even a place that holds memories you're ready to move on from. The practice allows you to regain balance by consciously severing those energetic attachments.

In a typical cord-cutting session, you begin by centering yourself and visualizing the energetic cords connecting you to whatever is holding you back. These cords could be tied to a person, a place, a past role, or even your old self. Once you've visualized the cords, the next step is to consciously "cut" them.

The practice is not about rejecting your past or forgetting the impact it had on you. Instead, it's about acknowledging what has run its course and releasing the emotional hold it has over you. For example, after the end of a relationship, if you find it hard to move on, visualizing and cutting the energetic cord can help you let go. Similarly, if you feel emotionally drained by a person or project, cord cutting can offer a sense of release and restore your emotional balance.

With respect to career crafting, this practice can help you move on from roles or identities that no longer align with where you would like to go. Whether it's a career path you've left behind, an organization you've outgrown, or an old version of yourself that you're ready to evolve from, visualizing and cutting those cords allows you to embrace the future with more clarity and freedom. It's a simple yet powerful way to practice emotional decluttering and step into the next phase of your life with more joy, ease, and possibility.

<u>Learnings from My Experience</u>

Engaging with energy and the invisible realms can be both simple or complex, depending on how deep you want to go. I hope I can find the right balance from my own learnings to share with you—I don't want to overwhelm you with too much detail that might make you shy away from exploring, but I also want to share some important tips and insights from my own journey. These include how to get the most out of whatever you learn, what to keep an eye on, and how to steer clear of a few mistakes I made along the way. It's easy to get caught up in the excitement and novelty of these practices, but it's equally important to approach it with discernment and a clear sense of what resonates with you. My hope is that by sharing these tips, you'll feel both encouraged and supported as you build your own relationship with energy tools, knowing that you can craft a transformative and enriching journey on your own terms.

1. Experiment, Experiment, Experiment

While theoretical knowledge is a great starting point, it's really the personal experimentation and experience that will actually give you a better understanding. Hearing about a teacher's or someone else's experiences can definitely spark insights, but let's be real—it only goes so far. Imagine this: you can read all about riding a bicycle and understand every little mechanic behind it, but until you actually hop on that bike and start pedalling, that knowledge is just floating in the air. It's your own trials and errors—feeling the balance, the momentum, and the sheer joy of movement—that really solidify the learning in a way that watching others can't.

Your hands-on experience is where the magic happens! You develop a personalized understanding that books and others stories can't teach, and those personal moments of discovery become part of your unique learning. Each experiment, each realization or feedback becomes a stepping stone, helping you refine your skills and deepen your understanding.

Your own experimentation is also important because we each connect with energy and the presence of our spiritual guides and angels in very unique ways. For some, it can feel like delightful vibrations; for others, it might manifest as warm or cool pulses. Some people 'hear' messages, others 'see' visions, and then there are those who simply know something is happening without any specific sensory feelings at all. There's just no one-size-fits-all approach to metaphysical learning and spiritual growth.

So, as you navigate your journey, put on your hat of exploration and curiosity, and start experimenting from day 1. Maybe set aside a few moments each day to reflect on what you felt or learned during your energy experiments. Keeping a journal can be a great way to track your progress, insights, and even those "aha" moments that often come when you least expect them. Personally, I've found that the lessons learned from my hands-on experiences far exceeded anything I picked up from books or the teachings of others.

Practice Trumps Knowledge

Here's a hard truth—we can acquire knowledge and even master various tools, yet still struggle to apply them effectively in our lives. This is true for biological habits like eating, sleeping, exercising, and also true for using energy tools. Having a deep understanding of metaphysical practices is a fantastic start, but without consistent application, their potential will remain untapped in your life (and career).

Think about it this way: you can have the best broom and mop available, along with a thorough understanding of floor cleaning techniques. You might even know the science behind why certain cleaning agents work better than others. Yet, if those tools remain stashed away in the closet, and you don't make it a habit to sweep or mop daily, your home will still accumulate dust and grime. You might wonder, "Why is my house still dirty when I have all the best tools and knowledge?" The answer is simple: knowing isn't doing.

The same principle applies to our careers and personal growth. We might read extensively about visualization, energy alignment, or setting intentions, but if we don't engage with these practices regularly, we risk falling into a rut. It's easy to feel overwhelmed or sceptical, especially when the results aren't immediate. The real magic happens when we cultivate a routine that incorporates these practices into our daily lives.

When you embrace these energy tools as part of your everyday experience, you'll begin to see how they can transform your career journey. Just as a daily cleaning routine keeps your home tidy, a consistent practice with these tools will clear the clutter from your mind and open up new pathways for growth and creativity. I have found that taking small but regular, intentional steps—whether it's a few moments of visualization in the morning or grounding myself before a class or meeting—can make a huge difference.

So, do remember that learning and understanding energy tools is just the beginning. You will reap the career benefits only of using them only if you make it a priority to engage with the practices regularly, and intentionally use them to help you in your career crafting journey. Remember, it's ultimately about taking regular action—about sweeping the floors of our minds and hearts and energetic fields to create spaces where our dreams and aspirations can flourish.

Karma, Free Will, and Black Magic

Let's chat about karma—it's a fascinating yet often misunderstood concept. The simplest way to look at karma is to think of it as a set of cosmic threads that weave our actions and their consequences together, constantly reminding us that every little thing we do matters. It's a gentle nudge to be mindful of how we show up in the world, and this is important even when it comes to our careers.

Let's bring in free will—while karma acts as a guiding principle ensuring we are accountable for the effects of our actions, we always have free will in every moment to choose our next steps. This is where many people get confused—believing that their destiny is shaped solely by past karma. They forget that even though the effects of past choices are something we must face, we are still free to make new, wiser choices in the present and future. These new choices create their own karma—hopefully beautiful karma, if we're making beautiful choices!

So, rather than seeing karma as a cage or prison, I encourage you to see it as an opportunity—an ally that ensures all your kindhearted and mission-driven efforts will bear fruit in the long run. And because even small shifts in our energy fields can create large, transformational effects in the visible world, remember the wise words of Spiderman: *"With great power comes great responsibility."*

Because energy tools are extremely powerful, it is even more important to have our ethics and values firmly in place when working with them.

On that note, let's bring in another highly misunderstood term: *'black magic.'* To understand black magic, we first need to understand 'magic.' Magic is simply a label used for things that are invisible or not explainable or exponentially transformational—and energy practices often meet all three criteria. 'Black magic,' then, refers to practices where energy tools are used with harmful intent, or to manipulate someone else. We can also enter grey areas when we try to influence others using energy tools—changing their preferences or choices, even if we think we're doing it for the 'right reasons.' Often we do this unintentionally, from a place of ignorance or ego, believing we know what's best for someone else.

I've made my fair share of mistakes with energy tools in my years of practice—remember I also started quite young. With all innocence, I've tried to alter another persons choices or thought I was helping or healing someone—only to later realize that I was interfering with their free will. In hindsight, I can see that ego, a sense of superiority, or incomplete understanding were at play each time, but I couldn't see it at that time. I did end up paying a price for those mistakes—but I learned some very useful lessons, albeit the hard way.

Now, I follow two simple guidelines (which you're welcome to borrow) to avoid stepping into 'black magic' territory. The first: Mind Your Own Business (MYOB). Use your energy tools and magic for yourself—your life, your body, your choices, your mission, and your dreams. The second: Highest Good of All Concerned (HGAC). When other people are involved in your intention or goal, always frame your ask with some form of HGAC.

For example, before I go into a teaching session, my prayer sounds something like: *"May this group (abc) learn and understand the topic (xyz), or whatever else is in their highest good right now."*

My goal in sharing all this isn't to intimidate you but to empower you. With a few simple guidelines, you can safely stay on the path of benevolent magic—spreading joy, love, and light wherever you go. And whenever you're unsure, call on your guardian angels. We all have them, even if you don't hear them right away. They never give up on us and are always ready to guide you, just like they've guided me through my own mistakes.

Remember to always view the law of karma as an ally, and let it work to help you. The law of Karma manifests through consequences (aimed to teach us), not as punishments aimed to make us suffer. The universe always has our back, and even when we think we are being punished, it is usually just a situation or a set of circumstances orchestrated to help us understand better, grow stronger or evolve further in our journey.

On the happier side, when you're crafting your career with purpose and joy, it's like sending out ripples of positive energy into the world. And just like ripples, they will return to you, often amplified. The more you align with benevolent intentions and take inspired actions, the more the universe responds in kind—opening doors, presenting opportunities, and attracting the right people and experiences your way. It's a dynamic process that keeps working behind the scenes to help you craft your career into a source of fulfilment and growth, not just for yourself, but for those around you too!

Fraudsters, Tricksters, and Scams

While we are on this topic, we might as well call out the big elephant in the room that's often on our minds when we talk about energy healers, coaches, and other practitioners of the metaphysical world. The question everyone asks—and for good reason—is, "How will I know that I'm not being exploited or taken for a ride?"

I really wish I had a concrete answer to give you, but the truth is, I don't. I do, however, have my own experience to share from over 30 years of being in this space. That's one of the benefits of growing older—you do tend to accumulate a lot of experience of all sorts!

I have crossed paths with people of varying degrees of integrity in all fields (from areas as regulated as banking and financial planning to areas like energy healing and psychic readings, which are far more intangible and difficult to measure). It almost seems to be a 'given' in our current society that there is generally a spectrum of human intentions and behavior in any field. At one end of the spectrum, there are people who are keen to exploit, brainwash and make a quick buck, while at the other end there are professionals who truly care and keep the client or customer's well-being at the center of what they do.

One thing to remember is that the more uninformed and uneducated you are in a certain area, the easier it is to get duped if someone is interested in deceiving you.

The second thing to remember is that the more we are afraid, or in a state of hopeless despair or desperation, the easier it is for us to get duped. When we are afraid, our reptilian brain takes control, and that is not the most intelligent part of our brain.

The third thing to remember is that the more desperate we are for something, the more likely we are to get duped. This desperation or urgency may not only come from fear of something unwanted but also from greed or excessive desire implanted in our brains. When our mind tells us, "Oh, I so badly want or need this!"—it becomes automatically vulnerable in that moment. Our desperation can also come from the fear of missing out (FOMO), because in this state, again, our reptilian brain is in control—it's just a relatively more 'exciting' fear.

The above three points are important to remember in order to maintain our inner sovereignty in any field—whether we are shopping for goods, jobs, vacations, medicines, treatments, or even just advice. Trust me, I my brain is as vulnerable to getting duped as yours and I have come up with these three points with lessons learnt the hard way.

A challenge with the energy and metaphysical field is that the first two factors are present in an exaggerated way. Most people are not educated and know very little about this space. Many also harbour some kind of fear of invisible forces or things they cannot 'see,' and this latent fear is easy to exploit.

The third factor—a feeling of "Oh, I want this so badly"—is also present in this field, and often the promises made by those offering energy tools seem too good to miss. And with good reason, because the results of working with energy can be truly transformational. We might have heard unbelievable and seemingly magical testimonials from friends or others who have used a service before us—and this possibility might over excite us.

In addition to the above three factors, what makes the metaphysical space even trickier is that the results are not easily measurable. Usually, they unfold over time, and it's difficult to make a one-to-one correlation between the benefit you received and the specific action you took—like clearing out an 'energy block.'

So how do we navigate this space? Here are my four bits of advice:

First, educate yourself at least a little on whatever service or modality you're seeking help with. Second, do a background check and ask for references you can trust whenever possible. Third, never make a decision or commitment when in a state of fear or panic (as much as possible). Fourth, always check your own excitement and eagerness levels for any change. Err on the side of believing that your brain is vulnerable to external excitement.

Let me share a little secret from my 30 years of communication with my own spiritual guides and angels. They are NEVER in a state of panic or despair. Even during my childhood fire accident and stampede experience, the voice I heard was calm, serene, peaceful. It was the tone a loving mother might use while giving a gentle hint during a jigsaw puzzle the child is solving.

My angels have never used the words, "Do this or else..." There are no threats, no ultimatums, and never a sense of, "This is your last chance to take up this offer." In thirty years, all I have heard from them are things along the lines of, "Unending hope," "All is well in the larger scheme of things," "Take it at your own pace," and "We are always here to help you". When they've nudged me to take action, talk to someone, start a project, or write something, it's always been suggested as a gentle possibility, and they leave me to choose. They've never highlighted the problems that might occur if I didn't go with their suggestion.

So when I seek out metaphysical coaches or teachers, I pay close attention to their tone in the first conversation. If I sense that they are planting fear, urgency, ultimatums, or "only this can save you" messages in my mind, I turn around and never return.

My final suggestion is to learn whichever modality interests you and practice by yourself—that's where the real fun lies anyways! And if you do need to get outside help, always keep your locus of power within yourself. Remember the Hero Mindset from Chapter 2? Never let that be taken away. The moment we slip into wanting to be "rescued" by someone else, we're giving our power away. While it's possible we may find a well-intentioned rescuer, we also open ourselves up to potential exploiters. Asking for help, assistance, and advice without losing your own internal power centre is absolutely possible—and that's the route I recommend as part of our inner sovereignty journey.

Why I wrote this chapter

This chapter was never intended to be a part of this book. Typically, I don't talk about energy practices or my spirit guides—at least, not outside the energy practitioner circles I'm part of. Why? Well, ever since I was a child, every time I mentioned these things, my family and friends would just roll their eyes. I've been surrounded by skeptics my whole life. So while I've always used these practices to enhance my work, I rarely speak about them openly. I don't teach them to my students or clients either, although I've occasionally incorporated them into private coaching sessions—only when a client was receptive to it.

The manuscript for this book was practically finished when life decided to intervene. One of my former students from IIMB, whom I had taught 12 years ago, reached out and asked me to conduct a workshop for his current company. After our Zoom call with his boss, he asked if we could chat for a while longer. That's when he asked me a question I've been asked before, but this time, he asked it with a piercing directness: "Ma'am, I've been following your videos on social media all these years. How do you keep your energy so high?"

I gave him my usual two answers. First, I'm not always in high energy. When I'm teaching or speaking about subjects I'm passionate about, my energy naturally spikes—that's what you see on social media. But there are plenty of moments when I'm low on energy, too. Otherwise, remember the basics: eat well, sleep enough, meditate, and exercise.

He nodded politely, but his gaze told me he wasn't satisfied. "Ma'am, there is something more to it..." he pressed. His persistence was undeniable. I made some excuse to end the conversation, but for the first time in a long while, I felt a pang of guilt. I knew I hadn't convinced him. I had told him the truth but not the whole truth. And he knew that I was holding back.

Later that day, I meditated and asked my spirit guides for guidance. Their answer was clear: "Share, but discerningly. There's no guarantee people won't mock you or doubt you, but you're strong enough now." I asked, "What about professionally? What if people stop working with me because they think I'm too 'woo-woo'?" My guides reassured me, *"Your clients come to you because of your deep intention to help them. Everything else is secondary. As long as your intention remains pure, your work will go on."*

And that's the conversation that gave me the courage to write this chapter. I understand it may not resonate with everyone, but if you've made it this far, perhaps it's meant for you! And before I end this chapter, I want to share answers to two more questions I have frequently been asked whenever I did try to share these practices.

Question 1: *"How can you be sure that this is not all just your hallucination?"*

Answer: So what is a hallucination really ? It is an experience involving the apparent perception of something not present. So given what I know (and what you also know after reading chapter 1 of this book), about subjective reality and the stories our brain tells us, we very well might in fact be always 'hallucinating'. Given this 'limitation' of our brain, if a certain 'hallucination' is helpful for me and helps me craft my life forward in a happy and contributive way, then I have no problem with it.

In fact, I invite you to think of the labels (or constructs) of God, or the Universe, or Angels, as yet another broad mental model that we hold in our brains. Based on these models our mind will make sense of whatever information it receives—whether it is in the form of visible signals and audible sound waves or invisible vibrations.

As long as the mental models that you are holding are helping you, I see no problem in it. If however you notice that your conceptualization of 'God' or 'Angels' or 'Energy' or a specific Energy Modality is getting you into a problematic place or it makes you passive and lazy, or other people exploit you, then it's time to relook at how you have defined these entities for yourself.

In fact a sequel to this book, could very well involve chapters that help us redefine our mental models of (and relationships with) God, with the Universe, with the spirit world and so on.

Question 2: If you know all these wonderful energy practices then how come your life is not perfect?

How come your body is not perfect? How come your relationships are not perfect? How come you still fall ill? How come you don't get everything you desire? How come you still experience challenges, crises, and failures?

Answer: The problem here is not with my body, my life or my relationships. They are fine as they are—because they are the beautiful 'work in progress manifestations' of my earthly journey. The problem is with your definition of *'perfect'*.

Think of an actual tree, a flower or a bird. Do they also have some of the problems that your mind categorizes as problems? Do they get hurt, or get diseases too? Our human lives are meant to be more like them and less like the 'perfect' plastic flowers or toy birds we see in shops. A 'perfect' human life is not one that has no problems or challenges or hardships. Rather these challenges and hardships are the gateways and teachers for us to learn and grow and evolve. This is why we spent an entire chapter on the Hero mindset and another on redefining our relationship with failure and resilience.

The aim of learning and practicing energy tools is not to try and 'eliminate' challenges and imperfections from your life. I assure you they will never go away. In fact as you outgrow the earlier ones, life will just lovingly hand you your next set of challenges—suited for the more resilient and stronger and wiser person that you have now evolved into.

Your energy tools and skills are just here to complement the other tools and skills that you already have been using on your hero's journey. Your angelic allies and guides are just here to complement your human allies and mentors who have been helping and supporting you all along. So rather than treating your growth and development as a finite journey with a 'perfect' destination, I would invite you to see it as an ever evolving *spiritual journey*, that your ever evolving *career crafting journey* is a subset of. And everything we talked about in chapters 1 to 12, whether it is about adopting a hero's mindset, redefining our mental models of specific constructs, dealing with failure, building resilience, navigating the inner critic, embracing the 'weirdness' of the unique person you are, setting goals, or managing conflicts—they are all applicable and relevant to your *spiritual journey* as well.

14

Fuelling and Fortifying Your Alchemy Process

"A mind that is stretched by new experiences can never go back to its old dimensions."

Oliver Wendell Holmes, Jr.

We've arrived at the final chapter of our journey together. In terms of your Hero's Journey, this is now the stage when you venture back into the Ordinary World. You take all the learnings, experiences, and revelations that you have picked up, and put them into practice.

Although, let me be more clear here. Though you're finishing one journey, you're at the threshold of starting a new one—the journey of crafting the next chapter of a fulfilling and rewarding career for yourself. Before you embark on this next phase, I'd like to leave you with a few more things that have made a huge difference to my life and career journey, and I pray that they will do the same for you too.

Deliberately Nurture an Appreciation Focus

As you embark on your career crafting journey, I want you to make a little pact with me—to keep a focus of appreciation[12]—with regard to yourself, your gifts, your progress, as well as the help and luck and support you might receive from outside. Now, why is this so important? Well here's a little secret: we're all wired to lean toward the negative. It's just part of being human. We're naturally more focused on spotting risks, anticipating what could go wrong, or dwelling on what already has, rather than celebrating what's going well or dreaming about future possibilities. And there's an evolutionary reason behind this negativity bias.

Imagine you're back in the days of our caveman ancestors, wandering through the jungle. If you fail to notice the pug marks of a tiger—well, that could be a fatal mistake. But if you miss spotting a new apple tree heavy with fruit or a beautiful rainbow arching across the sky, it's not as critical. Sure, missing the apples means you go without a tasty snack, and missing the rainbow means you lose out on a moment of wonder or inspiration, but your life isn't at stake.

To increase our chances of survival, evolution programmed our brains to focus more on problems and potential threats than on the positive things around us. That's exactly why we need to intentionally practice appreciation.

In fact, the word appreciation has two meanings to it. First, it means recognizing the good qualities or benefits of something or someone (and yes, that someone can be you!). Second, it means to increase in value. When it comes to nurturing the new you, both

---

[12] If you want to know more about the science of appreciation please refer to the book resources website.

meanings are spot on. The more you acknowledge how your new belief systems, behaviors, or patterns are helping you move forward, the more value you'll start to see in your new path. And guess what? The more confidence you'll have to stick to it.

And here's the magic part: the more you stick to your new path and work on it, the better the results you'll see. Remember the self-fulfilling prophecy we discussed in Chapter 1? Over time, you'll realize that you're not just moving forward—you're creating incredible value for yourself through your efforts during this career transformation journey.

So let's make sure we're not just surviving this process, but thriving in it by consciously looking out and acknowledging all the luck and support that comes your way, as well as the amazing strides you yourself are making.

Dealing with Friends and Family

When you're on a journey of personal growth, it's important to be aware of how your progress might ripple through your relationships—especially with those closest to you, like your spouse, children, and dear friends. Every relationship tends to 'settle' into a certain rhythm, a pattern of give-and-take, and a certain level of emotional dependency that seems to work for both people involved.

Now, whether those patterns are healthy or not, they're still patterns, and any shake-up in them can feel a bit like stepping into unknown territory. It can be unsettling, even for the most loving of friends and family members, who might start—perhaps without even realizing it—nudging you back toward your old self, the version of you that felt comfortable and familiar to them.

So, what's your task here? It's to be ready for this, to stay alert for any signs that your loved ones might be feeling uneasy about your changes, and to hold your ground gently yet firmly as you work on these inner or outer transformations you're embracing.

Here's a little imagery that helps me: Think of when you plant a young sapling in the ground. You surround it with a little fence, something to protect it from being trampled by cattle or damaged by the elements. Once that sapling grows strong roots and starts maturing into a sturdy tree, the fence isn't necessary anymore. Even if cattle come by and nibble on its branches, the tree is resilient enough to sprout new growth and keep thriving. I remind myself of this every time I'm making a significant shift in my inner or outer world. In those early days of change, I know I need to take extra care to protect and nurture the new belief system I'm cultivating or the new routine I'm trying out. And interestingly enough, sometimes I need to shield this newer version of myself from the very people who love me most. But once the change takes root, I can let down my guard and allow my relationships to find their new balance, a new pattern of interdependence that works for everyone.

Another thing to consider is the influence of the wider circles, groups, and conversations that fill your daily life. Sometimes, when you make a big shift in your inner world, it might be time to step back from certain circles and step into new ones that align better with your upgraded belief system. Otherwise, you might not be giving your new belief system the nurturing it needs to survive, especially amidst the flood of opinions and judgments from your previous groups - and yes, I am also talking about your many Whatsapp groups here!

Don't let your Professional Self Image trap you

We all carry around a picture in our heads of who we are—our self-image. It's like a mental snapshot that captures how we see ourselves, what we believe we're good at, what we value, and what we do. Remember the 'Tree of Life Diagram' you created in Chapter 9? One of the key reasons behind that exercise was to help you consciously craft a resourceful and empowering self-image. But here's the thing: none of that is the absolute truth. We are far more complex and limitless than any single image could ever capture. Think of these self-images as mental models that we use to navigate life, and the key is to make sure these models are lifting us up, not holding us back.

Ideally, your professional self-image should be like a high platform—a launchpad that enables you to leap, soar, and thrive. It can empower you to work better, contribute more meaningfully, support others, achieve abundance, and live a fulfilling life. But here's the flip side: if we're not careful, that same self-image can become a prison. Instead of being a platform that helps us grow, it can trap us, keeping us stuck and limited.

Let me share a story from my own experience. When I first became a professor, I believed my role required me to strictly stick to peer-reviewed science and conventional academic methods. Even though I had a deep interest in philosophy and other spiritual modalities, I kept those aspects separate from my work because I had this rigid idea of what a professor "should" be. That narrow mental model of my 'role' held me back from innovating and integrating new possibilities into my curriculum.

It was one of my coaches who helped me realize that I had unintentionally created a cage around myself by clinging too tightly to a narrow definition of my professional identity. She literally asked me, *'Ramya, why are you keeping your magic away from your students'.* This was a wake up moment for me and from that day I began to allow myself to create new and innovative exercises that integrated tools and wisdom from many different fields and modalities.

Ultimately, your self-image should serve you and your work, not constrain you. Don't turn it into a prison, rather, and let it be a platform from which you explore new possibilities and grow into increasingly more impactful versions of yourself.

Promoting Yourself (And Your Dreams)

In life and especially in your career, the support of others is invaluable. They can create opportunities, place you in the right positions, and help you do your best work. But for this to happen, they need to know about your strengths, talents, and potential. That's where self-promotion comes in. It's not about being boastful or arrogant; it's about letting the world see what you have to offer. When others recognize your light, they can open doors that you might not even know were there.

I understand—self-promotion can seem daunting. You might worry about coming off as arrogant. So, let's explore some ways to ease these concerns.

First, focus on the value you offer rather than just talking about yourself. Self-promotion is really about showing how your skills can benefit others. When you approach it from a service perspective—thinking about how you can help and contribute—it feels more natural and less self-centered.

Next, consider self-promotion as a win-win situation. By showcasing your strengths, you attract opportunities that align with your skills. At the same time, you make it easier for your colleagues, employers, collaborators, and clients to leverage your abilities, which ultimately benefits everyone involved.

Also, think about the impact of your self-promotion on your network. Sharing your achievements and goals is a way of acknowledging the support and guidance of mentors, friends, and family. As someone who's both mentored others and been mentored myself, I can tell you that seeing someone you've supported succeed is incredibly rewarding. It's a shared victory that reflects the collaborative effort behind personal growth. So shine your light bright, not just for yourself, but to honour the efforts of all those who've helped you become who you are today.

And as you are promoting yourself and your work, don't forget—your dreams deserve to be out in the world as well, not tucked away in a corner. When you share your visions and aspirations, you open the door for help and resources to flow in from the most unexpected places. How will you know who might become a collaborator, sponsor, donor, funder, supporter or mentor if you're too shy or scared to share what you're working towards? Of course, you can be mindful and judicious about who you share it with, but don't let fear hold you back. Often, the right people and opportunities seem to find their way to you when you dare to speak your dreams into existence.

What I have further discovered is that the utility of sharing your dreams isn't just about attracting the right people or opportunities—it's also about reinforcing your own commitment to them. When you articulate your goals and visions to others, you're not just informing them; you're also reaffirming to yourself that these dreams matter. This act of voicing your aspirations can ignite your own motivation and make your dreams feel more tangible and within reach. Plus, you might inspire others in the process—your courage to share can become the catalyst for someone else to pursue their own dreams. So, don't underestimate the power of speaking your vision out loud; it's a powerful step towards making it a reality.

Empowering Yourself with People Skills

Working with others is an essential aspect of nearly every career—even in freelance roles like mine. So whether you're collaborating with colleagues, leading a team, negotiating with clients and vendors, or engaging with stakeholders, your ability to work effectively with others can make or break not just your professional success but also how much you enjoy your work itself. Unfortunately, most conventional curriculums do not teach people skills in schools. That's why many people like me have it really rough when we suddenly transition from the world of books and machines into working with people.

The inner work in this book is about managing yourself—that too managing your thoughts mostly. And that is indeed extremely important (and an absolute game-changer). However, I do want to let you know that while an inside-out approach begins inside it need not end there. Please keep learning, and continuously upskill yourself with people management knowledge and practices. This is a vast curriculum that I now have deep respect for, and even though I have a PhD in Organizational Behaviour, for me the learnings are still progressively sinking in with each new day of real life experiences. Your own experiences will teach you too - but this learning can be accelerated when combined with the frameworks and best practices of people management.

The good news is that there's a lot of relevant research that has been already done on these topics—and its all waiting to be mastered by you. Emotional intelligence can help you read the room, manage your emotions, and respond with grace. Effective communication is about much more than clear speech; it's about listening deeply and ensuring your words truly connect. Conflict management can turns friction into moments of growth and learning and negotiation skills can help you transform haggles into creative opportunities for mutual gain.

You can think of mastering these topics as the building blocks for creating work environments that are dynamic, joyful, productive and rewarding. The more you learn, the more you empower yourself to create spaces where you and those around you can genuinely connect, grow, and thrive together.

Choose Your Scope and Pace of Crafting

Scope: As you work through this book, you'll engage with questions, exercises, and tools - all designed to shake up your inner and outer worlds. For some, this might lead to massive life redesigns. I've seen past participants in my programs switch careers, commit to moving countries, or leave their current jobs to embark on full-time educational adventures. But not all transformations are visible. Some participants haven't changed anything on the outside but have experienced profound inner shifts. For instance, there are those who ended the program with a rock-solid commitment to work on their inner voices or those who've now made it an ongoing mental habit to flip perceived problems into opportunities. Imagine, for example, someone who enters the program feeling like a 'failure' only to leave with a newfound awareness that they've always been a prototype in the making—learning and evolving all along.

The way you engage with the exercises in this book is entirely up to you. How your transformations manifest will be as unique as you are, shaped by your current situation, constraints, and personal priorities. There's no hierarchy of importance between inner and outer transformations. Both are valuable and contribute to your journey. Often, one type of change will set the stage for the other. Sometimes, an inner shift will make the external changes easier, and vice versa.

Pace: Here's a little secret: you're actually the best judge of not just which path to take at what point, but also how fast you want to travel on it and recognizing this is an essential part of your inner sovereignty.

It's easy for our brains to get caught up in the "faster is better" trap. But remember, that sense of urgency can be a sneaky trick that pulls us off course. In fact our brains are particularly more vulnerable to suggestions that contain within them a sense of implanted urgency (as we saw in chapter 10 when we discussed goal setting).

So while I encourage you to set goals and milestones for yourself as you work through this book, please do it in a way where it creates an optimum level of motivation, excitement and engagement. A pace that delights you and fills you with the joy of living, a pace that challenges and engages you, but not a pace that frustrates you and throws you into overwhelm. Your journey is definitely not a rat-race—but it is not a race of any kind at all—just a delightful, evolving adventure, with many nested *'heroes journeys'* in it!

And on the cusp of your own exciting journey, I'd like to offer you a token of inspiration—a poem I penned ten years ago that has since become my daily anthem.

~ I Am the Canvas ~

I came face to face with God
I could not believe my delight
Finally today would be the day
I could end my arduous fight

I pulled out my list of wishes
I pulled out my list of complaints
I handed them over to God
To His angels and His saints

God took my list from me
And lovingly went through it
And with an amazingly tender smile
Said, "You have misunderstood it"

"You've got this game a little wrong"
He said with a mischievous grin
"It is not one of seeking treasure
And checking off how much you win

This is a game of creation
And we are all co-artists here
Just go ahead and paint your dreams
Which you have held so dear"

I looked around for brushes
I looked for paints and pencils
I asked if I could get a canvas
I asked for tools and stencils

God smiled at me once again
With the radiance of the Sun
He said to me, "You are the canvas"
He said, "You are the One"

"You are the painter, you are the paint,
You are the pencil you need
You are the glitter, you are the glue
You are the paper and bead

You are the craftsman, you are the wood
You are the potter and clay
The field of consciousness in your head
Is your playground upon which to play

Go paint your dreams in that space
And craft your ideals there
Your body, your life, your own conduct
Is the art you have to share

I am with you, I am in you
We are strung together in love
We are creators all creating together
Some on earth and some above!"

-Ramya Ranganathan

Epilogue: Doing what you like or liking what you do ?

I remember my early attempts at working—each one a disaster in its own unique way. Even though the memories have lost their sting, I can still clearly recall how I felt at the time.

I remember sitting on the 18th floor of a plush office, gazing out at the beautiful blue Arabian Sea stretching endlessly before me. The vastness of the ocean was a stark contrast to the sense of contraction and confinement I felt in my job. I wondered why I had let myself be trapped in a work routine that felt like a prison. Did I dare step out? Was my paycheck high enough to bribe my body into sitting cramped at a desk from 9 to 5 for 25 days a month?

I remember staring dumbfounded at a report I had painstakingly prepared after a week of work, only to be told that I had to re-analyze the data and recreate it so that a downward-trending graph would instead show an upward trend. My boss literally screamed at me, "Ramya, if I submit this report, I'll lose my job." I thought about all my school math teachers and wanted to tell them that the math they'd taught me hadn't prepared me for the corporate world. Here I was, being asked to use a different kind of math—decide the desired trend first, then create logic and input to support it.

I remember hiding and crying in the bathroom (almost daily), so nobody saw my emotional and vulnerable side at work. I was one of only two women on a whole floor of open-plan offices, and I cringed inside, but outwardly, I faked a smile whenever a male colleague stomped across our office floor using foul language or making obscene gestures. This was the accepted 'office culture' on that floor of the bank where I worked, and it almost felt like being inside a men's locker room where people were trying to show off their wit and courage through sexually charged language and actions.

I also remember the incredibly long hours I spent on work and commuting each day. I clocked precious moments of my life at a desk that felt like a prison—sometimes because of work piling up, but many other times just because it wasn't acceptable to be seen leaving the workplace early. My goal was to reach home by 10 p.m. each night so I could catch an episode of Friends and laugh along with the characters on TV, just to feel a little lighter. But deep down, I was miserable. I didn't know why I was doing what I was doing— except for the fact that everyone around me seemed to be doing something similar.

I hated my work. But when I complained about it, many people told me I needed to practice acceptance, to make peace with my circumstances and find a way to like whatever job I had. In short, they told me, "Happiness lies in liking what you do, not doing what you like."

I had heard this saying before, and I hated it. A poster in my mother's bedroom bore those exact words, and had I read it every day growing up—and every day, it had angered me. It felt as if this saying was asking me to compromise, to just make things work, no matter how bad it felt. It felt like it was taking away my freedom to choose better places and jobs to work in, ones where I could thrive. I became a strong champion of the "doing what you like" (DWL) philosophy. This was in stark contrast to not just my mother but many others who tried to convince me of the merits of the "liking what you do" (LWD) approach.

Even as I went on to study and research the person-work relationship, I initially focused only on how to help people find the 'right fit' or 'right career.' Over the years, I crossed paths with many people, both in academic and philosophical circles, and we spent countless hours debating whether happiness lies in liking what we do or doing what we like. Even in my research on careers, I found two separate camps. The DWL camp advocated discovering one's inner passions, interests, and strengths, then finding a career that accommodated those. They emphasized searching for jobs based on the environment you liked, activities you enjoyed (or didn't), and the people you wanted to work with.

The LWD camp, in contrast, took a more Eastern philosophical approach, highlighting the importance of 'fitting in,' 'making do with what's available,' and 'using every experience as an opportunity to grow,' even if the experience was unpleasant.

Given my interest in Buddhist philosophy and my own growing practice of meditation and inner work, I began to slowly see the wisdom in the LWD approach. Yet I could not fully accept it either. I lived with this internal struggle for many years, until the universe finally orchestrated a customized learning for me, something I fondly refer to as my Himalayan Learning Experience—which I share below, along with its back story.

The Himalayas will Make me Happy

When I was about 13 years old, I had gone on my first Himalayan trek. I remember the first night up in the mountains at our base camp when I was sitting on a rock beside the stream looking up at the stars, amazed that there were so many stars in the sky. Living in the city, I had never seen a sky so full of stars. I felt an incredible mix of happiness, peace, awe, wonder and expansiveness — and this became my new benchmark for how amazing life can feel.

In my mind, I concluded that there was something special about the Himalayas, something magical that could only happen there. I dreamed of going back, but life kept intervening, and I could just never make it. I went trekking in other places and even in other countries, but I never made it back to the higher mountains of the Himalayas.

So I kept waiting for an opportunity to reconnect with that same depth of peace and happiness that I had once experienced at the age of 13. I firmly believed that "the Himalayas will make me happy."

Finally, in my thirties, I had a chance to go back. I was so excited, so eager, believing that I would find that same happiness and peace again. We landed in an extremely remote village high in the Himalayas, surrounded by majestic mountains. But I didn't find the bliss I was craving. The more I didn't find it, the more anxious and irritated I became. I was finally back in the Himalayas, but the peace and happiness I expected wasn't there.

One morning, I set out on a walk while everyone else was still asleep and wandered into a nearby monastery. The monks were chanting together in harmony, and it was incredibly beautiful. I sat with them for a while and got engulfed in the peaceful vibrations that they were creating. As I walked back, I reflected on their disciplined routine of working on their inner spaces.

That was when I had my BIG aha moment! It occurred to me that if peace and happiness were only about being in the Himalayas, then these monks wouldn't need to wake up every morning to chant and work on their inner mental spaces. Suddenly, I realized that finding peace and happiness required more than just a conducive environment—it also depended on training the mind. The monks were using both the DWL and LWD approaches. Sure, the

Himalayas provided a conducive backdrop for experiencing peace and joy, but the monks were also doing daily inner work to create and sustain that bliss within and around themselves.

Combining the Two Approaches

The more I thought about it, the more obvious it became that a hybrid approach between DWL and LWD wasn't just possible but practical. When discussing this with colleagues in the career research space, I began using an analogy to explain it—a physical health analogy. If we want to stay healthy, most of us don't debate whether it's more important to build immunity or maintain hygienic surroundings. In an ideal scenario, if we had total immunity (absolute inner strength), we could theoretically swim in a garbage dump without getting sick. On the other hand, if we could perfectly sanitize our surroundings (find the perfect job fit), we might not need to worry about building our internal immunity. But most of us live in the real world, not these extremes, so we do both to the best of our ability. Doing one doesn't mean we can't do the other. There is wisdom in combining both approaches, and we can use this combination to experience better mental and emotional health while working.

The inside-out approach I've outlined in this book will help you shape your career in a direction where you do more and more work you love (the DWL approach). Yet, I encourage you to also build strong LWD muscles. I have already nudged you along this path by encouraging you to include growth and learning as desired outcomes in your personal Return on Time Invested (ROTI) list at work. Another strategy is to remember that any task, if structured with clear goals and feedback, can be gamified to make it more enjoyable and even lead to a flow state. The key is to keep adjusting and raising the challenge level as your skills grow—just like they do in video games.

No matter how carefully you choose your job, environment, and co-workers, there will always be some amount of unpleasant work in any job. But it's possible to train our mind to deal with it, to bring enjoyment, focus, and satisfaction into what might otherwise feel mundane or overwhelming. I too have my own share of such tasks as part of my work. Things like accounting, making proposals, grading assignments and some other things. So even though you might be doing what you like in a more general way there are likely to be smaller tasks within your job where you need to bring in your inner LWD muscles. I like to think of these as the 'diaper changing equivalent' tasks within a career that we love. Most parents do not intrinsically enjoy changing diapers. Yet we willingly do it because we see that task as an integral and required part of bringing up the baby that we love so much. Or travel? We might love exploring new places, but there's also packing, security checks, and long waits at airports. The things we love are rarely perfect packages, and that will be true for the work and career that we love as well. They are likely to come wrapped in duties, tasks, and sometimes even drudgery, but we still choose to embrace them because they're part of something bigger.

And finally, let's not forget the super driving force of purpose. Whether you're doing what you love or learning to like what you do, your purpose can be the thread that ties it all together. Your purpose can help you navigate the tougher days, ground you when tasks feel overwhelming, and remind you why you're showing up every day.

Afterword : Role of Leadership & Culture

Our work can indeed be our best friend or our worst enemy. My mission is to empower as many people as I can to experience their work and their career as something that is meaningful, engaging, enjoyable and fulfilling. This is the driving force behind creating the Career Alchemy Process you've explored in this book.

While this process is incredibly powerful and can lead to remarkable transformations, it's important to recognize another key element: for those working within larger organizations or under the direction of a leader, their experience is also heavily influenced by how their manager nurtures, supports, and guides them. An organization's culture can significantly impact a person's overall work experience, as well as the shaping of their mental models about key things like success, work, failure, conflicts and growth. A leader or managers behaviour can also influence a person's own self belief in himself or herself through the Pygmalion effect.

This realization drives my two-pronged approach to fulfil my mission of de-villainizing work as a lived experience in our society. On one hand, I work with individuals to empower them from the inside out, as we've done with this program on career alchemy. On the other, I collaborate with leaders and organizations through workshops and trainings, helping them craft workplaces that are truly win-win. One where both the employer and the employee recognize the value they bring to each other and are mindful about making this synergy work for the highest good of all concerned.

With this objective I've been conducting leadership workshops on the following topics.[13]

1. Personal Mastery for Leaders
2. Growth Mindset
3. Psychological Safety
4. Managing Conflicts
5. Innovation Mindset
6. Emotional Intelligence & Managing Stress
7. Cultivating Inner and Outer Resilience
8. Design Thinking
9. Leading with Joy
10. Change Management
11. Crises Management
12. Win-Win Negotiations
13. Owning your Voice
14. Mission, Vision & Values Alignment
15. Accelerating Women Leaders

If you're a leader who shares my mission I would love to connect with you. Together, we can co-design a workshop or learning journey tailored to your organization's unique needs. We really need a cultural and social change to transform what the world of work can be on our planet—and we can make this happen, one organization at a time, one team at a time.

---

[13] You can find a list of client organizations at <u>www.craftingourlivescom</u>

Acknowledgments

To my students, participants, coaching clients, and online readers —this book would not have grown without your inputs, your interactions, your efforts in efforts in doing previous versions of the many exercises in this book and your growth, which became the inspiration to write this book for a wider audience.

To my teachers, guides, mentors, and angels—Deepest gratitude, for your inspiration, knowledge, support and wisdom. I walk my work with confidence only because I know you have my back, and you work *through* me and *with* me in every piece of teaching, speaking, or writing. Listing and enumerating each one of you would be another book by itself, but I have cited your contributions wherever possible. For the teachers I have not directly cited, your teachings have made me who I am today, capable of paying your love forward through the writing of this book.

Sai, this book would not have been written without your love, motivation, and belief. Your refusal to let me get away with writing shorter posts and articles finally paid off. Sid, because you thought I will never finish this book - I just had to! Thank you for challenging me with your impish smile.

Mummy and Daddy, I am me because of your nurturing and unconditional support—you remain an inspiration to me, at every turn and bend of life. Kavitha, just knowing you are a phone call away, has kept me going on the bleakest of days, Ramya (N), how did I get so lucky to find a friend to share not just my heart and soul with, but also my name, and Zara, our walks have sustained me through the toughest phases of this writing marathon.

References

Chapter 1: Getting Started with Inner Sovereignty

Exercise #1, Data Gathering: Modification of an exercise done at London Business School taught by Prof Srikumar Rao.

Pygmalion Effect: Rosenthal, R., & Jacobson, L. (1968). Pygmalion in the classroom: Teacher expectation and pupils' intellectual development. Holt, Rinehart & Winston.

Chapter 2: Your Career as a Hero's Journey

The Hero's Journey: Campbell, J. (2004). The hero with a thousand faces (3rd ed.). Princeton University Press.

Growth mindset: Dweck, C. S. (2006). Mindset: The new psychology of success. Ballantine Books.

Ch 3: Unpacking Success & Personalizing It

Write Your Own Obituary: Modification of an exercise built on an earlier version that was part of orientation at LBS.

Interesting Point of View: Tool from Access Consciousness

Ch 4: De-Villainizing and Redefining Work

Flow State: Csikszentmihalyi, M. (1990). Flow: The psychology of optimal experience. Harper & Row.

Return on Time Invested: Gallwey, W. T. (2000). The inner game of work: Focus, learning, pleasure, and mobility in the workplace. Random House.

Ch 5: Integrating Money, Work & Service

Money EQ: Honda, Ken, Happy Money: The Japanese Art of Making Peace With Your Money. New York, Gallery Books, 2019.

Ch 6: Manoeuvring your Lizard Brain

Attention Deficit Trait: Hallowell, E. M. (2005). Overloaded circuits: Why smart people underperform. Harvard Business Review, 83, 54-62.

Ch 7: Navigating Failure & Cultivating Resilience

Circle of Concern: Taylor, Jane. "The Circle of Concern and Influence." Habits for Wellbeing. https://www.habitsforwellbeing.com/the-circle-of-concern-and-influence/

Victor Frankl: Frankl, V. E. (2006). Man's search for meaning: An introduction to logotherapy (4th ed.). Beacon Press.

Resilience Network: Cross, R., Dillon, K., & Greenberg, D. (2021). The secret to building resilience. Harvard Business Review.

Ch 8: Co-Working with Inner Voices

Inner Critic: Paul, L. (1970). The cruel inner critic. Psychotherapy: Theory, Research & Practice, 7(3), 178–180.

Inner mentor: Mohr, T. (2014). Playing big: Practical wisdom for women who want to speak up, create, and lead. Avery.

Imposter syndrome: Cuddy, A. J. C., Wolf, E. B., Glick, P., & Crotty, S. (2005). Imposter syndrome and how to combat it. Harvard Business Review.

Inner Child: Bradshaw, J. (1990). Homecoming: Reclaiming and healing your inner child. Bantam Books.

References

Ch 9: Leveraging Your Unique Weirdness

Asch Experiments: Asch, S. E. (1951). Effects of group pressure upon the modification and distortion of judgments. In H. Guetzkow (Ed.), Groups, leadership and men (pp. 177-190). Carnegie Press.

Tree of Life Exercise: Modification of exercise learnt from Coach For Life Foundation, by Peter Redding

Ch 10: Using Goals: A Double Edged Tool

Effects of Goal Setting: Ranganathan, R., & Dagar, C. (2017). Savouring the journey: Key to leveraging the double-edged sword of goals (IIM Bangalore Research Paper No. 535)

Effectuation: Sarasvathy, S. D. (2008). Effectuation: Elements of entrepreneurial expertise. Edward Elgar Publishing.

Ch 11: Portfolio Careers for Multipotentialites

Ikigai: García, Héctor, 1981-, Francesc Miralles and Heather, Cleary, Ikigai: The Japanese Secret to a Long and Happy Life. New York, Penguin Books, 2017

Multipotentialite: Wapnick, E. (2017). How to be everything: A guide for those who (still) don't know what they want to be when they grow up. HarperOne

Ch 12: Managing Conflicts Along Your Journey

Types of Conflict: DeChurch, L. A., Mesmer-Magnus, J. R., & Doty, D. (2013). Moving beyond relationship and task conflict: toward a process-state perspective. Journal of Applied Psychology, 98(4), 559.